Another Day to Love

Sunday Morning Ramblings

Another Day to Love – Sunday Morning Ramblings
Copyright © 2019 Kolein V Carlson

ISBN: 978-1082705151

First printing November 2019
in the United States of America

Cover Photography & Design: Kolein Velvette Carlson
Lilac Tree in Highland Park, with Nikon DX

www.freetofindpearls.com
Free To Find Pearls - Art - Song - Story - Spirit
Facebook & Instagram

This book is dedicated to the man I share coffee with every morning, and to our sons. None can compare.

Introduction

Leaving people we love can sometimes mean we find our true selves.

Writing about the experience is a surefire way to that end...or perhaps a new beginning.

I canNOT imagine what shunning is like for the shunner. It must be like riding the biggest wave of arrogance in a moment. I will LOVE the shunners anyway. They are sad and afraid and cowardly and weak. How can one not feel empathy for that state of being? I am over the hump, 10 months out. The reality is we have moved on or are trying to move on. While extremely difficult, the lessons are hard fire lessons that burn and mold one's soul into grace and care and understanding. Gentle is the way for me. Love is truly the only answer. It began that way 15 years ago stepping into that building. Never a drop of regret truly loving those people. But love has left the building. And love is light and it cannot occupy the same space as the darkness of arrogance. This is no easy feat. I am after all just a girl living life in a creative way, loving her sons and her husband and her friends. Lies are whipping around about us making their way into our lives. This is truly challenging. I won't deny that. However, at the end of every day, I am thankful that oppression is no longer a noose swinging near and around me or my children - one I had to continually avoid for true fear of spiritual

death. #theotherside #nolongeraslave #lovetrulysaves
#meanpeoplearebroken

After exiting the only church I'd ever served or spent time with, my Sundays were now free. I had no idea exactly just how free they were or how free I was becoming. The beginning of this healing process ended up becoming one of the most important pieces of my life long metamorphosis. I had no idea who I was at 35 – when I entered such a place, such a stage in the growth of my character. But I knew I had to become someone. The residual tarnishes of a broken home and meandering young adult life had me in a constant state of misunderstandings – mine and everyone else's. I will never look back on that time or those decisions with remorse. They brought me to myself. Not everyone gets to say those words. By 49, I was hearing the soft whispers of a trapped child. It was saying, "Leap of faith or choke to death? You choose."

While this story appears to have its beginning with the exit of a fundamentalist church that is by no means the true beginning.
As you read the ramblings many ideas are regurgitated, formulated and acknowledged. They come from the depths of a searching soul. Seeking truth has become a popular culture catch phrase. Finding it is another matter all its own. Then, what do we do once we have the truth right in front of us? I chose to love.
This is my journey.

All these ramblings were typed out in the moment. Very rarely did I edit or alter any of them. That raw honesty HAD to be there and I knew it. Otherwise, I'd be just like the rest of the angry/hurt world digging deeper into a pit of darkness and staying there, grabbing others down with me. I was crawling out toward the light. No easy feat. This free-flowing expression is where my heart travels. I allow that for myself whenever I write. With each numbered rambling there was a slight pause where inspiration could have its say. I allowed that as well. So this is a compilation of those words written on Sundays, with one or two on a Saturday or Monday. I had no idea I was writing a book as I typed out these ramblings. I was writing myself out of the darkness, the pain by pouring love into all of my wounds. What began as a heartbreaking ending in August of 2013 eventually became, through the voice of inspiration – which for me is audible – a book with a voice by August of 2019.

What I found is that writing is healing. I didn't know that until I started writing, then healing. We often hear the suggestion, "Journal your feelings, thoughts." I'm sure that changes us, too. I've been "a writer" since I could write. Penning my feelings, ideas is just part of the day. However, I had no idea when I sat at my laptop on Sunday that my ramblings would be the solace, the punching bag, the balm my heart and soul needed; not to mention the push my ego required to tumble off any cliffs of the ego-self. These ramblings remain a piece of me, exposed to the reader, yes, but mostly to myself. Carefully placing these words "out there" nearly each week was/is therapy. This collection expresses a broken-to-bits heart and offers each of us a way out to create a light-filtering mosaic in our own lives. We must allow the light in. Otherwise, we remain in the darkness. Period.

Honesty is a treasure. It is not always treasured by those around us. Following our inner-voice, our guide, our gut, our God is going to make waves. As it should. The waves will either be the storm or they will be a navigational instrument. They were both for me. Calm waters. A peaceful shore. I eventually arrived there. The realization that the lighthouse, the beacon is within means I no longer drift aimlessly through this world.

My hope is that a few of these words mean something to you, to your heart and perhaps even your soul.

Thank you for being here. It means we get to be together.

Kolein

With a closer look, what I thought was a chain around my wrist

was but a shadow.   Freedom.

Kolein Velvette Carlson

You may not control all the events that happen to you, but you can decide not to be reduced by them.

Maya Angelou

2013

Ramblings:

1. No.

2. No.

3. No.

4. All the good words have NOT been taken.

5. Maybe I should sew?

6. Or paint?

7. I think I'll write.

December

Sunday Morning Ramblings: December 2013

1. So many deep feelings around writing about my experience of being shunned for these last few months of 2013. I don't clearly know whether to do it. And yet, it seems it would be the most healing act.

2. It's such a delicate matter. I love those who are shunning me. And would never, ever mean to hurt them. Yet the pain that their cultish beliefs have ensnared them in is causing this behavior.

3. This form of bondage is still occurring today. I posted this because you, my dear friends who know what has happened to us, have loved and cared for me and my sweet family during such a time.

4. I would appreciate some of your thoughts and feelings about this.

5. And to those who may not know the details, please feel free to comment as well.

6. No matter what has happened I still believe LOVE is all around.

7. Written with a heavy heart. We left in August.

8. It took me until December to begin to write about it.

9. I was in a heap on the floor until then.

It's Sunday. Another day to love. Happy Sunday

Sunday Morning Ramblings: December 2013

1. I used to have this group of friends. They'd come over and play and laugh and create and eat and cry and talk for hours on end.

2. Then I left their religion - the one that said they LOVED everybody, no matter what.

3. This religion created hypocrisy and insecurity and hate and anger and arrogance.

4. I had to leave that.

5. It's contrary to who I am and who I'm always hoping to become.

6. Those "friends"? Nowhere to be found.

7. I still hope for them. I still care for them. I hope they read this.

8. I hope they know that our hearts are still *for* them. They know who we are. They know in their hearts that we, my husband and I and our boys, could NOT stay in something that was a lie.

9. I would like them to know that there is a better, safer, purer way to love freely, honestly without the trappings and chains of men's hands and indoctrination. #heartsturnedtowardlove #freedomfromreligion #warningsallaround #outsidethebuidling #fourwallsdonotdefinelove #itisatrap #ImgonnaLOVEyouanyway

It's Sunday. Another day to love. Happy Sunday.

To find yourself, think for yourself.

Socrates

The individual has always had to struggle to keep from being overwhelmed by the tribe. If you try it, you will be lonely often, and sometimes frightened. But no price is too high to pay for the privilege of owning yourself.

Friedrich Nietzsche

2014

June

Sunday Morning Ramblings: June 2014

1. Bike riding to me is much like flying. Always has been. It represents freedom and a perspective that one never gets walking or running. I love it with my whole self. Except for one time when a bug flew into my mouth and lodged itself just past my epiglottis, thus throwing me off the bike into the nearby grass, choking and coughing and nearly vomiting. That was 6th grade. I am, however, still an avid bike rider, mouth closed.

2. People all over the world today are worshipping a man named Jesus. Wonder what he would say about it?

3. I choose love over most stuff. Pretty much always. Is that a middle child thing? I'm not a middle child.

4. I dream way more than I DO. I wish it wasn't like that. Sitting here for the past week recuperating made me think about this dreaming. Well, I was dreaming and then I realized that since I couldn't do anything, I was dreaming a lot. Not more than most days, just without the interrupting thoughts of chores and questions/answers that are prevalent in my days of doing while dreaming.

5. I like Facebook. I know there are questionable things about internet stuff. But I choose love, even on FB. I don't read the news. Only the good stuff. I'm not an Ostrich.

6. My sons listen way more than I think they do. I had this awakening once again last night. I love awakenings. I never think I'm perfect. But what I realized is that they forget, get distracted. But listen. They do.

7. My husband is still the love of my life. He is truly one of the greatest men I have ever known. He's intelligent and funny and kind to literally everyone. He doesn't small talk or cheat anyone out of deserved care in the moment. We are home together all day long, pretty much every single day. He's retired (4 yrs) and I'm a stay at home mom. It works. It's lovely. And we have a little house. That's love.

8. My friends are gorgeous. They have shown me more Christianity (which to me, is defined as LOVE) than people I used to worship with. That has been a massive eye opener.

9. I don't worship anything or anyone anymore. I believe it's wrong to do that. I love. I love my neighbors. I love my enemies. But worship isn't correct. I'm thankful. And grateful. Forever. But worshipping people, no matter who they are in present time or past seems to miss the point. But I do love. And that keeps me grounded and present. It doesn't put me in another state of mind, which is not reality. It keeps me here where I'm needed.

10. I don't judge people anymore.

11. I am judged and gossiped about more than I would ever have believed in my entire life. All of the gossip is made up manipulated lies by the leaders of a place I used to trust, when I

was in another state of mind. That to me is very mean. And hurtful. But I figure God must want me to know or at the very least, it gives me something to learn. We have virtually no contact with any of the members of *that place* and yet we keep learning about the lies they are spreading. EC says it's perfect. (I love him) He says we get to truly love those who despitefully use us.

12. I forgive people. For real.

13. I miss my dad. He lives over an hour away. Because of his troubles and family issues, I don't see him much. He's 81. A cowboy. He was my first hero.

14. Crying heals me.

15. I'm a writer. Of words. Musings. Poetry. Short Stories. Songs. I used to have trouble saying that. I turned 50, had my entire world turned upside down. Now I'm ok with saying who I am and what I do. No one can rob you of YOU.

16. If you are in a place where there is a bully - someone who is trying to control your life in any way, take heed to this idea: If you believe in God and HE doesn't control you, but gives you FREE WILL, why would you turn your life over to a bully to do that to you or a group of people? Just think about that one. Why are YOU subjecting yourself to such treatment? True freedom requires no master, no slavery, but the voice within to guide you. Why isn't it enough to trust that voice?

17. Ending here.

It's Sunday. Another day to love. Happy Sunday.

Life shrinks or expands in proportion to one's courage.

Anais Nin

July

Sunday Morning Ramblings: July 2014

1. I prefer to let people be. I think we receive the best of everyone if there's space for each of us in the room.

2. I try to be aware that I don't take up too much space.

3. I like not having a gall bladder.

4. I'm growing my bangs/fringe out for the 700th time.

5. My friend's daughter just had a birthday. I was with her when she took her first steps, 26 years ago. Somehow remembering that makes me oh-so happy!

6. I don't feel older, overall, only certain bits. I still love running and racing down the big hill in Mendon Ponds Park and cannot help myself from laughing each and every time.

7. I love my neighbors at our little end of the street. They are good and kind.

8. I find peace in the breezy, gray days, like today.

9. I spent Friday evening with some of the most amazing women I could ever know. We've known each other since we were young teenagers in school. When I woke the next day I missed them all and recognized that they were missing.

10. I'm going to try really hard to have them over today before we all disperse from whence we came.

11. Love is big and can reach across a great divide as long as there is someone at the other end with their heart stretched out to meet yours. Otherwise, the echo is painfully thunderous.

12. We need each other, for many things. Just remember, the color wheel is giant and not everyone should meet every need, nor be required to make your gray yellow or your blue pink.

13. I like being alone in unfamiliar surroundings.

14. I was just eating rapturously delicious blueberries. Then the bite of mold stole away my euphoria and I was grateful for spitting. We can be grateful for bodily functions, if we choose. #olderbrother

15. I read a lot. Everyday. Might be why my house isn't as clean as it could be. Or maybe not.

16. I don't think having a clean house matters as much as we think it does. I try not to think about it.

17. Amazing how perspectives change. I used to hate my house. Now I love it. I used to think it was "way too small." Now it's the perfect size. I used to think I was fat when I was a size smaller in high school and now that I've lost all the pregnancy postpartum peri-menopause weight I feel slimmer than ever. Perspective ROCKS!

18. I compared myself to a tree the other day while on the phone with a friend. It was a special moment for me.

It's Sunday. Another day to love. Happy Sunday.

To be nobody but yourself in a world which is doing its best, night and day, to make you everybody else means to fight the hardest battle which any human being can fight, and never stop fighting.

ee cummings

August

Sunday Morning Ramblings: August 2014

1. I turned the oven on this morning...for heat. I wasn't sure if that was "the right thing to do" so I decided to make brownies. It's an electric oven. Not gas. I did not stick my head inside. Making brownies is always the right thing to do.

2. Before I married I was the best of friends with a gay man. We were in many ways closer than I have ever been with any man, other than EC. Sharing our life stories. I know this man's heart. It's tender and kind and forgiving. Living in fear of judgment or having to "fight" it off is a terrible place to try to exist. Don't hate gay people. Please don't reject them. It's like breaking the heart of a child over and over and over again.

3. It's much easier to love. Don't believe me? Just try it for a bit.

4. Okay, this is the thing. I believe it's time to bring back our joy. Stop kicking it to the curb as though it's interfering with our pain. Pain is the boss? Come on! Please! It can't be. One thing for sure, and we all know this to be true, we've got pain...all sorts of pain, all colors, varieties, flavors. I've got pain. You've got pain. Heart aches and muscle aches and brain aches and thought aches and so many aches. It's as if we're running around scared of this pain that's going to come at any moment to wreck our lives. Friends, family, acquaintances, we have mastered pain.

Masters of it. Masters of the Pain Universe. All of us. It does not matter which variety intensifies your life, you are currently holding the world title in it. So. Instead. Let's talk about a little drop of joy today. Just a little, okay?

5. Possessing joy does not alter, for instance, the fact that, Robin Williams died. Or anyone else we've known or loved has died or suffered. We suffer plenty. Masters of it, remember? So how about going out and finding some joy. Yeah. It's got to be found. No one, as far as I can tell, is giving it away. But if someone has it and you're looking for it, guess what? YOU WILL FIND IT! Folks, however, do try to sell it. But we already understand we can't buy joy, love, or any of the really cool and flavorful jelly beans in the jar. The only way is to find it. Look for it. It's all around. It's free. It's yours. Mine. JOY.

6. I'm realizing the foul stench of religion that tries to rear its ugliness into my life via people is based wholly on their own internal fears and doubts and literally has nothing to do with me. Being shielded from the attack is my greatest challenge. No. Actually not retaliating is.

7. No one knows your heart, unless YOU express it to them. And even then, there is a beautiful mystery so deep within. Take care of that special spot. It's truly all we have.

8. EC and the boys woke up early and went fishing this morning. I merely woke up early.

9. We've been at the lake house for one whole week of 7 days. My cellular being, my emotional being, my gypsy being, my poetic being all agree that we don't want to leave, just yet.

10. I've awoken to my self. I was familiar with her before coming to the lake. Let's just say I'm getting reacquainted with her mind, her body and her soul.

11. My passion is being freed. *tears

12. The boys' boat is close enough that I can hear them. They all just let out a great exclamation of "Oh my gosh, that's HUGE!" EC is laughing. I like to refer to them as "fishers of fish."

It's Sunday. Another day to love. Happy Sunday.

Fear is the cheapest room in the house. I would like to see you
living in better conditions.

Hafiz

September

Sunday Morning Ramblings: September 2014

(it's not morning here, but it most definitely is somewhere else)

1. I love LOVE it when EC and the boys go out of town to the mountains. LOVE IT! Three days. LoVE it!!!! Girlfriend reunions. Open spaces of time and thought and eating. Walks, strolls, heck I even take the time to brush my hair instead of the scrunch of the curls. Low stress. No stress. Busy catching up on....eVeRyThInG! Day dreaming, sleep dreaming, dreaming dreaming and then, it hits. The other love thought. Usually comes after the "good night Mommy!" over the phone.

I LOVE it when EC and the boys come home. *choked tears

2. I don't involve myself or my thinking in much to do with politics or rallies or bandwagons or food companies or the like, because I firmly believe in relationship, one-on-one as the breath and life of our day to day, but I do have a question. Why are so many people pretending? What happened to being real? Kind? Generous? Oh, I know and I mean, I KNOW, kindness exists and generosity is prevalent, but what happened to folks, companies, politicians, CEO's, teachers, store owners, the pizza guy, the dentist, friends from high school, bloggers? When did everyone stop being who they really inherently are to then pretend? Why isn't it comfortable to be BE BE ourselves? Why are so many

running around playing pretend as liars keeping truth at bay and literally and purposefully lying to themselves, others, the world. When did decisions get made to provide false information, or incognito ingredients or developed panels of experts barfing up "a story" to keep the public in the dark? What is this mass produced psyche-trap that we've gotten ourselves into? It's like a collective schmooze of some ill fate, sickening, hurtful, disgusting, rub penetrating deeply into the layers of our beautiful dermis. Food companies tricking people. Politicians tricking people. Store owners tricking people. Magazine companies tricking people. So many manipulators. A collective sad fear wide spread for what? A piece of the pie. Lose your soul, not to mention all the other stuff, so you can enjoy that sliver of sweet flaky crust and fruit filling, alone? Alone. Yes, selfishness produces loneliness. Forever. Manipulation equals ALONE. The view from the mountain top is pretty amazing. But sit there by yourself, no one to share it with and after a bit...well, you just might need to climb down.

3. Ok, now I've started....yikes. Bullying of any kind comes only ONLY ONLY from fear. I don't believe in puppeteering. I don't believe GOD is the master puppeteer pulling our strings getting us to do what HE wants. I believe we do what we want or what we believe we are supposed to do in any given moment. Is there some kind of intervention ever? Have you been privy to any personally? Whatever your answer, go with that.
Faith. Not religion. Not the Bible. Not the group. Just simply faith. Live by that.

And love. Above everything else, love. It will never hurt you. Love people where they are at. Love where you're at. Not a drippy love. A real, understandable love of allowing yourself or others to be who they are. If they hurt you more than once, deliberately, you then have a choice to make. If they believe in games, other than the ones on a board, well, you have a choice to make. It'll be ok. I've lost several hundred people within the last year, as well as a handful of relatives and former friends. Starting over is never easy. You have to admit, though, there is a certain amount of effectual exhilaration attached to the idea!

4. Being better equipped to love several people MORE PROFOUNDLY from a distance produces less stress lines. Although you may have more laugh lines! There are creams for that. Everybody wins!

5. These are ramblings.

6. I don't eat much sugar. Not from some earth shaking decision made one day in a violent purge of all sweet products in my home; merely a transforming letting go. I hardly crave the stuff anymore. When I eat it, wow! It's tastes so incredibly yummy!!!! And sweet. Very sweet.

7. I love my friends. They are true. I don't label them. Whatever their beliefs, they are their beliefs. I love them for who they REALLY are. The truth in them is a much more profound beauty. I enjoy breathing in that beauty.

8. Walking is good. Running is faster. I do both. Not at the same time. That would be silly.

9. I hope my friends who call themselves Christians don't feel marginalized because I don't follow dogma or laws or labels or words or ideas or a cross. Interesting thing is that after attending a church for over 15 years I never once thought of myself as a Christian. Not once.

10. And speaking of religion, our next door neighbors could be called Hindus. I like to call them "the most lovely people" next door. They share their festivals and holidays with us by dancing on their deck, smiling and loving each other donned in stunning apparel, sharing what the earth has produced from their gardens, not to mention the most mouthwatering home cooked Indian cuisine that could make a heart sing Hallelujah like Pavarotti.

11. I find that without all the singing and constant praising and altar calls and shouting from the platform of a church I see, feel, notice more...God, my surroundings, my self, others and words, trees, my breakouts, my 10yo's little boy-ness, the smell of food, my husband's smile, the 6'2" height of my 13 yo, my toenails. And space. There is more relieving space to be...in. All of that kind of partying is good for a time. I think. My time was so up.

12. Today on my way home from the farmer's market I took a different road. It isn't necessarily the one less traveled but I don't usually go this way home. I'm happy to report that I saw something that made me smile and transcend driving. (I like to get out of the mundane while in the midst of the mundane).

Stopped at a traffic light, I hit the radio station to change the channel. Lovely Irish music filled the car! Several folks were crossing at the crosswalk. I looked at the two young men crossing (it's a college town here). No doubt good friends probably going to get some lunch. They were going eastward. Westward came another young man. His gait was fluid and confident and secure. He didn't walk too fast or too slow. He was determined, yet without arrogance or pointed focus. Carrying his backpack, short cropped hair cut, handsome face, deep eyes...and then it happened. I was in Dublin. My God! I kid you not. I was transported, right there, in my car. I was certain that if I rolled the window down to say, "Hey", to that young man, he would have spoken with an Irish lilt.

13. This is my life. Welcome to it.

It's Sunday. Another day to love. Happy Sunday

Sunday Morning Ramblings: September 2014

1. Drawing from the joy of the past, let's talk about yesterday. I began the re-creation of a piece of furniture that has been walking its way around my house for years, as a basic-wooden-wannabe-mini-farmhouse table. EC and I carried the table out front to our patio. It was exhilarating! Yep. Carrying a table out the front door = exhilaration. EC began sanding the top while I worked in the yard with the boys picking up branches and sticks. Then I began weeding the front garden. The boys walked the

dogs, then went on to a friendly toss of the football. Brightly colored mums were scattered here and there in a wagon and baskets, as the hum of the sander played its melody. As "work and play" commenced, my hands doing one thing, my mind envisioning the transformation of my basic-wooden-wannabe-mini-farmhouse table. One could say I'm talented that way. I would say I'm more of a blend of creative ingredients in a Kitchen Aid mixer, just as the start button is hit, bits flying all over the place. Tabletop sanded. Lunch is made. I grab some paint for the legs of my basic-wooden-wannabe-mini-farmhouse table. Old fashioned-farmhouse house grey (I made that up. It was $1 oops sample at HD). I'm smiling the entire time. I'm painting. Yep. Painting. I smile some more. Then a friend of the boys joins us for the afternoon. EC takes them go-karting. I've been commissioned to Target to replenish the boys' supply of Nerf darts for their next phase of play – Nerf gun "war." This is perfect. I can grab some wheels for my basic-wooden-wannabe-mini-farmhouse table as well as the clear coat at HD then pick up the meatball subs on the way home. After unloading the goodies I walk out onto the patio and stare at my basic-wooden-wannabe-mini-farmhouse table. I love it. It's not done yet. I love things even when they're not done. Laughter and chatting is heard from the family room, then a mad dash outdoors ready for Nerf play, the boys are "having the time of our lives" - to quote our 10 yo. I get choked up. *tears. Yep, having the time of our lives.

2. Speaking of the past, last week I was battling with resentment. I won.

3. I like myself. A lot. Don't you? I mean, don't you like yourself? A lot? If you don't here's my number: xxx-xxx-xxxx. I'll clear up any messes, misunderstandings, confusions for you. Don't waste a second not liking yourself. And if you can find it in your heart, try to love yourself. The world around you will be a better place.

4. I like you.

5. I wouldn't be sitting in my bed writing this right now if I didn't. Earlier I was sitting in my special quiet corner in the living room writing this (where I write just about every morning – MOMMA NEEDS HER QUIET TIME, PEOPLE!) but the house woke up early and I had to run away into my boudoir. So I'm writing here thinking of you.

6. I like you.

7. Schedules have changed here this fall into what appeared at first glance like the innards of the Kitchen Aid mixer. I was scared. Then I was offered to do the books for an artist friend for their artist guild. I said No. Honestly, I think it's the first time I honored who I really am without apologizing for not being everything to everyone every second of every God loving minute of every friggin' day. I'm not a bookkeeper. I would cry rivers of tears if I had to do that. Rivers, I tell ya. I can count and teach mathematics to my boys, but ladies and gents, I am not interested in spreadsheets. Oy. Someone get me a stiff drink. Kidding. (I

don't even know what a stiff drink is.) So, I said, no. It didn't hurt anyone. No one died in the making of this decision. And. And. The reason my friend thought to ask me to help out with the bookkeeping was because as she put it, "the only requisite was that the person be honest and I thought of you." *tears

8. OK, back to schedules....geesh....I tell ya with these ramblings; schedules. Well, we're finding our new rhythm. It's good. It's busy. They're boys. Busy is good for boys. And they get to be quiet and slow, too. That's a good mix. I was the one all in a huff about it. More work for Momma is usually not a nice thing to do. But it's not more work. It's actually different work. I was resisting change. Me? Can you believe it? Me? Change-o-rama woman, resisting change? I got over myself after three weeks.

9. I like being married. It is an institution. I'm good with that. I looked up the definition of institution. This was the most poignant definition: an organization providing residential care for people with special needs. That fits. Don't ya think?

10. I love laughing. My friend, Beth posted last night, "I just want to spend the rest of my life laughing." I laughed so hard. In fact, I'm laughing typing this.

11. I want to plan a trip to a Country Living Fair. Who wants to join me?

12. Don't forget your magnesium. Seriously. If you take calcium, Vit D or any of the B's, you need magnesium to process those vits in your body. Otherwise they dump somewhere else or don't do a thing for you. We drink ours. It helps relieve

muscle cramps, anxiety, nervousness and a whole bunch of stuff. My favorite is that it helps me sleep deeply. Read about it if you have the time.

13. Shelby Rae! Hi! Just in case you got this far. Love you. Can we have lunch together soon?

It's Sunday. Another day to love. Happy Sunday.

Fear defeats more people than any other one thing in the world.

Ralph Waldo Emerson

October

Sunday Morning Ramblings: October 2014

1. I lived with irrational fear while attending that place. That is the design. I thought about going into therapy over this ugly cult thing I was blindly led into. I'm still thinking about it. Right now, guess what? This is my therapy. I realize all the philosophical truths - "a lump of clay has to be in the fire before its beauty can be revealed", "lessons are painful", "there must a reason." yada yada yada. However, every day a new truth, a new awareness gets uncovered. This is healing me, because I realize where the pain is coming from and can put a salve on that particular spot. I'm not in a heap on the floor any longer. Although, I still have issues. I still hurt. I can only compare it to one of my closest and dearest friend's divorce. He walked around in a fog for years trying to piece together the semblance of a life. He went to work every day, spent time with friends, even laughed but his heart and mind were always underneath the thick cover of a life he had lived, wondering if he'd ever be happy or truly live again. I hope you don't think I'm weak for still feeling this. I need real people now. The kind that have been through the fire themselves and can grab my hand and pull me out with love. Love will be the only way.

2. I'm not in THAT place up there, #1, all the time.

3. People should pay for their actions. But they don't. So I must move on.

4. Nearly 30 people have exited *that place* in the past year. I hope they are truly free.

5. When a slave gets set free I wonder how long it takes for freedom to settle in?

6. #2 seems in error. Trust me, it's not.

7. Ramblings, remember? Oh and this is my therapy. I'd journal but no one would ever read it, including me.

8. You can turn this thing off at any moment.

9. This is not a drama. It's real life.

10. I'm a singer and a songwriter. I hope (and pray) I have the courage some day to express that piece of myself with you. 15 years of fear does a number on a person.

11. I need you.

12. I need me.

13. I'm not depressed. Just rambling.

14. You can't fix this or me. I'm rambling, remember?

15. You are my new community. I decided I really needed one. Thank you for being here...with me.

16. I was missing high school friends the other day something fierce. Maybe that's the reason for the reunions. Although it's never exactly what we want, those reunions. I think I'd prefer to have everyone over my house for a big dinner and a sleepover for the entire weekend, maybe even into Monday.

17. I'm hoping to paint on canvas today. But first we've got a piece of furniture to buy for our 14yo's room. Then it's complete. It's important that we keep our promises to each other.

18. My page is public now. So I'm going to take a wild gander that dear folks from that cult church are reading it. You probably don't know completely but you are suffering greatly being bullied into a part of something that is the BIGGEST FREAKIN LIE walking.

It's Sunday. Another day to love. Happy Sunday.

I will not hide my tastes or aversions. I will so trust that what is deep is holy, that I will do strongly before the sun and moon whatever only rejoices me, and the heart appoints.

Ralph Waldo Emerson

november

Sunday Morning Ramblings: November 2014

1. If there is the proverbial box I'd like you all to know we have officially kicked it to the curb. The whole thing. This world around us is amazing. Don't get locked into a belief system. LOCKED. You will have built your box and will have to fight internally, extremely hard, to stay there as well as convince everyone around you that it is THE BEST BOX IN ALL THE WORLD. #noboxes

2. I drove by *that building* the other day. I felt nothing. But a confirmation of peace and relief. I took notice of all the people working there...running ragged serving, serving, serving, trying to get into heaven, being bullied, etc.   It's a choice. They chose to stay.

3. One of my former closest friends from *that building* is engaged to be married. Her parents were close friends of ours, too. They live out of town. We found out months ago from a mutual friend. This engaged friend used to be at our house all the time. For over 10 years, closer than family. And now nothing. That's a psycho-religion. It's not what Christianity is or claims to be. It's not even what she wants. It's not even human. She's just too afraid to see the trap for what it is. I love her so very much. #caredeeply

4. If there is a stubbornness in you, you are not free. At all. Let it go.

5. These are ramblings.

6. This is my therapy. I've paid for other kinds of psychological and emotional therapy before. I'm sure it helped me in some ways. However, writing this to all of you is instant help, instant healing.

7. Speaking of therapy, I did improv the other night. For real. I used to be funny, before *that building*. I was in a funk for months and I asked the Universe/God/Jehovah/aliens/spirit/butterflies/fill in your favorite, what I should do? The answer was to do improv. I know, right? Who in their right mind does that? (nobody answer that please) So. I went to a workshop. And jumped in. People laughed. And I lived. #drovehome #thehappiestIhavebeen #inthelongest15yearsofmyentirelife

8. We've been completing many projects here at our house. We have time now. Imagine that. It's not being eaten away serving a thief. #letsbehonest

9. Sometimes our own personal honesty when it is expressed may appear raw or out of line to others. Whatever anyone thinks, it remains honest.

10. Cognitive Dissonance. Look it up. It blew my mind.

11. Now that I've expressed so much I need to say this, I am changed forever. I'm sorry for those who remain trapped in that cult. The words may seem harsh, but the heart is tender.

12. My husband, EC, plays the harmonica. Sets the room on fire with it. If you need to feel some freedom, ask him to play for you sometime. You'll be changed. And glad you listened. I posted a video on Friday.

13. My freedom and self-awareness and inner love is an unfolding of many trials and deep wounds. I don't think there is any other way. #keeplovepresent

14. I miss my friends who live all across North America. Can we just plan a party and all meet up at some neutral destination? Of course we can. Who's in?

15. Thank you for being here. You make a difference.

It's Sunday Another day to love Happy Sunday

Sunday Evening Ramblings: November 2014
(ramblings happen any time of the day or evening, don't you know?)
1. We have no plans for Thanksgiving.

2. We did put in our turkey order. Tom will be arriving early this week. I'll cook him when I feel like it. #holidaysequalcalmness

2.5. We have a bird man.

3. Since "losing our religion" (how many of you thought of REM's song after reading that?) there are no more traditions. We are thinking of converting to FREEDOM, instead.

4. On my bookshelf (hold on, if I gave you that list...hmm...too transparent), really what I mean, near my bed, sits Ralph Waldo Emerson and Henry David Thoreau. I thought it only fair and kind that I finally read their essays, in their entirety. I've been carrying and posting (with real paper) their words around just about every desk I've ever had for the past 30 years - home or work or both. Now. It is time to read the other sentences attached to ones that have become wise, reassuring friends.

5. I think I've written or at least thought many of the words Emerson has written. It's wild. Really. We are one in words and spirit. Or maybe they just simply speak to me.

6. I've learned Louisa May Alcott's (Little Women) father - also part of the Transcendentalists - didn't really work and their family suffered greatly at the lack of his responsibility.

7. Let's talk for a moment about responsibility. I used to think responsibility was a thorn in my side. I hated to "have to" do anything. I "wanted to bang on the drums all day." I was taught completely wrong. When I met my husband - long before we were married - he taught me how to climb a mountain. A real

one. A high peak in the Adirondacks. Really, Kolein, you had trouble climbing a mountain? Well, I learned on snow shoes, you see, in the middle of winter. Traversing over creeks and branches as I ascended up. a. mountain. I kept whispering through sweat and tears, "I can't do this!" He kept saying, "Yes, you can. One step. Then the next." Eventually we made it to a clearing. I sat and cried. I did it. He did, too. EC was wearing cross country skis. Climbing a freakin' mountain on skis! He taught me how to stand on my own two feet and walk, one foot in front of the other, taking careful steps. That example of triumph taught me to never give up on the climb. I refer to that real life example a lot in my real life FULL and overflowing with responsibilities. The mountains we climb in our day-to-day lives, if we continue "one step, then the next", will get us to the clearing. And it will be gorgeous and worth it!! <3

8. I love people. Still. Even after all of THIS - deception, meanness, theft, cruelty, abuse, etc. I still love people. The people in my life are so incredible, so unique and perfect. They remind me of the REAL GOODNESS that remains, and never gives up or gives in.

9. Did you know that many of the holiday/seasonal songs we are listening to this time of year were written by Jewish folks? Just sayin.

10. I like to call myself a HUMAN BEING now. It gives me a tickle and a wonderful feeling joining me to all the other HUMAN BEINGS around. You are a human, if and only if, you know it. Otherwise, you might call yourself something else.

11. As I was typing this I looked over at my music collection to the left of my page and saw Sting staring at me and thought he was listening in on what I was writing. Ha. He's got that eavesdropping look on his face.

12. Did I ever tell you that many years ago I saw Sting when he was "just Sting" not Sting and The Police? The show was at an intimate venue in NYC. We arrived early. Then we snagged front row, standing in front of the stage "seats." At one point Sting was singing out and sprayed us with his saliva. That's right. Splash! Right on our faces! I was completely grossed out. It might be a great story if I was a bra-slinging groupie. But I'm not.

13. We saw Bill Staines (singer/storyteller/guitarist) the other night here in our city. We also sat in the front row. No saliva. It was good, clean fun. The boys have been listening to him since they were born (maybe even before that). They both play his songs on the guitar. There was a guitar giveaway at the CD table. A man came over and encouraged them to play it. What we didn't realize was Bill was standing there listening to them. Our 11 year old played Roseville Fair. Our 14 year old played River and Piney River Girl. He talked to them afterwards. Music is universal and gorgeous.

14. While typing this I ate a bucket of popcorn- bigger than my head bucket.

It's Sunday. Another day to love. Happy Sunday

It takes a man to suffer ignorance and smile.

Gordon Sumner

December

Sunday Morning Ramblings: December 2014

1. If I can sit and talk with honest people. Real people. People who risk and breathe out their story to fill the room, not with details, but with expression so pure a heart would sing and eyes would soften and tenderness reaches depths unknown...that is what it IS all about for me and my life. #truthforms

2. Let's talk about teenage boys. I mean really...with all their energy and kind spirits and athleticism and smarts and how they still say, "thank you" and "please" even though they stand over 6 feet tall and have a clear view of the part in my hair, let's talk about this. #whoselifeisthis #momsofteensweighin

3. I believe our physical selves have some form of knowledge and memory. How many times have I gotten up to walk into a specific room or area of our home to realize my body knew something my brain did not? So. I stand and wait. When my brain catches up, my whole self is now in on what it was supposed to be doing. #bodymindmeld

4. I also believe that our brain can do amazing feats, while leaving our body completely out of the equation. If they were to collaborate on certain things I know that our bodies would rebel, "put their foot down." Examples are catching a falling baby or glass jar or running down the bleachers at my son's basketball

game and across the court to give him a water bottle to then run RUN back in front of the folks sitting on the bleachers then up those bleachers to sit down. Clearly there was no collaborative effort. I just did it. My brain was completely in charge of this one. #justdoit

5. Every third day or so I run around the house and open just about every single window. Then I have a cup of tea, sit for a spell, then run back around and close them all. #lettinggoofstaleair

6. I adore a good metaphor.

7. Cinnamon buns fresh from the oven elevate serotonin levels. #IamaBiologist

8. One and a half Christmas trees are up. All the lights we bought last year only work on 2/3s of each string. Yet, the lights I've had for about 12 years work and are brightly lit. #newjunk

9. I don't usually do words for the year. If I were to list a few right now off the top of my head for 2014, they'd be:
anger
frustration
envy
doubt
loneliness
realization
purpose
and
direction

All of that up there is necessary to get us going...somewhere, very fine.

10. We are learning and uncovering so many new ideas and historical facts about the design of religions all over the world. It's fascinating and exciting and bewildering all in the same moment. #neveraconvert #loveistheonlyanswer

11. Leaving no space for people to be who they are is one of the greatest atrocities in life. Parents have this privilege. Friends have this privilege. #weareNOTallthesameperson #becomeAWARE

12. I love art. I am art.

It's Sunday. Another day to love. Happy Sunday

If God had wanted me otherwise, He would have created me otherwise.

Johann von Goethe

2015

January

Sunday Morning Ramblings: January 2015
(began writing this Saturday afternoon)

1. I love being loved. I hope I love as much as I'm loved. There is nothing sweeter than having someone I love tell me, show me, surprise me with their love for me. It's never grand or display worthy or shiny. I'm pretty simple in the love-need department. Low maintenance has claimed its place for me. Just a hug. Or a touch. Or warming up the car. Or saying "thank you, Mom." Or a text from a friend. The word love doesn't need to be part of the expression. I was acknowledged for being an artist by my best friend, who I happened to have married. That's what began this thinking about how much I love being loved.

2. I've also been thinking about how many dear people go through life, large portions of it, without a touch or expression of love. Several come to mind. They have pushed people away perhaps. Fear, self-hate, whatever the cause, created a void. Now the very people they have pushed don't want to express love toward them. It's a tight knot someone has to begin untying, hopefully, at some point.

3. Eleven year olds are very wise. They are transitioning from baby/young'un to a separate being. They notice everything about this transition. They may even keep us up at night. They

cry a little more. And fear a little more. And worry a little more. They make decisions. And hold the large jug of milk, without spilling. They may speak wisdom in a burst of anger. I was struggling with this transition. Then I sat one evening in the dark, watching the embers in the wood stove. Wisdom was given to me. "He's wise. Listen up. Take notice. But keep reminding him that not every thing is full of drama." I'm wondering if that drama part was meant for him or me.

4. So. Here we are. Our sweet family making our new life out of a place that tried to claim our lives. It didn't. My 11yo wants to know why we keep talking about it. I told him, "So we can get through it." His thought, "We are already through it. We were in it. Now we're out. We're through it." #wisdom

5. Pay attention to people smaller than you. They've got words.

6. I decided to believe in God. Even though I can't prove a darn thing. It doesn't matter what anyone thinks about it or me. #experiencedthedivine

7. I miss my friends who don't live in this area anymore. If we were to move we'd have to purchase too many houses in order to spend time with them. #agirlcandream #anyoneupforawinnebagovisit

8. I've found that writing about the people in my life shows me a depth in relationship that I would not see otherwise or may forget some days.

9. I like you.

10. Making a place for peace is important to me. When the boys were little we had Quiet Time every afternoon. Then it became Momma's Tea Time. Now. I just leave the house. #lol

It's Sunday. Another day to love. Happy Sunday.

Being deeply loved by someone gives you strength, while loving someone deeply gives you courage.

Lao Tzu

February

1. Beliefs are just that...something you believe in? I think in Western culture we are taught arrogantly and misguided into the belief systems we have to endure. I say, endure, because they make me tired. So tired, I want to cry. Sitting at the table at a family function we were discussing whether or not a man named Jesus was really on the earth in his miraculous form. Just discussing it. (My husband and sons and I have been diving into the history of religion for a while now.) We've uncovered some really amazing findings. But just the mention of such an idea caused one of our family members to stubbornly raise her hand in my face and say, "I don't want to hear it. Jesus is who I believe in. I'm not talking about this with you." Why? Why not uncover the truth? Isn't that ultimately what we ALL hope for? Maybe not. I don't blame her for being afraid. I completely understand that fear. (trust me) Why the fear? Why the stubbornness? My short answer is: religion. It gets in the way of love. It gets in the way of relationships. I know. I was in relationship to hundreds of people. When I stopped believing in their religion they stopped talking to me. And put me on some imaginary blacklist. LOVE is BIG, friends. That kind of behavior is fear. So back to the family member. She hasn't been around lately. That's OK. The confusion begins with what the religious world calls

"separation." However, love doesn't separate. She really loves us. However, her belief system is in the way for now.

2. I would like to thank my Christian friends here on FB for not shunning me. I know at times there must be a challenge of sorts because none of you comment on my ramblings much. However, I love you for who you are...NOT EVER for what you believe. #friendsforever

3. Why are so many people in the Western Christian world going to underdeveloped countries thinking they have ALL the answers about God for people who are just trying to get clean water? They need water. Perhaps that IS their salvation. Notice how no one is going to a lawyer's coop or doctor's office or business club to try to save anyone? It seems like the seemingly vulnerable get that offer all the time. True love has no need for control or manipulation. I believe that truth is in the bible. And last I knew, we were NOT supposed to judge. So if you're deciding who the "lost" really are...yikes! Playing God is a big shoe to wear.

4. Before EC and I were married he went on wilderness trips A LOT. Work kept me from joining him and also the whole bug and dirt thing, being outside all day and night, etc. etc. But I wanted him to take "me" with him. So I gave him a little rubber eraser shaped like a cute cartoon-like angel. He put that in his pocket on all his travels. And seriously that little guy is still in his winter gear jacket today. (23 years later) Did I really go with him on those trips? Nope. Was I in the lodge with him sitting in

front of the fireplace? Nope. Did I really ski down mountains next to him? No. But in spirit, in thought, in his heart, I was there with him. Some would call that little gesture of love (the angel eraser) the anti-Christ. Is anyone following me with this?

5. When the head of a church meets with individual members and lies about someone who has left and the reasons they left, is that illegal? #deepsadnessaboutthisone

6. To my knowledge, I've never rejected anyone EVER based on their belief system. I sat among a church of Christians and never believed I was one. I was there for LOVE.

7. We don't really know anything for sure. Except a few things. You can create your own list.

8. I'm so glad to be connected with authors, artists from all over the world here on FB. Seriously. The joy is unbelievable!

9. Interior house paint is in my future. Eeeek

10. Had a brownie with berries dumped on top for breakfast.

11. Coffee can be a savior. #mynewbeliefsystem

12. If someone were to ask me what I believe in...my answer would be love, first. Next would be good food and honesty, in that order, because no one can ever lie in the midst of a good meal.

13. I love people. Except for people who lie about me. Then I find it extremely hard to love them. I feel sorry for them. Even if

they are leaders in a place called *a church*. I still feel deeply sorry for them.

14. These are ramblings.

15. What's on my mind is NOT always what's in my heart. Today I'm very, very sad.

16. I met with a friend for coffee this morning, on one of the coldest, slippery-est, freezing-est days of this winter. It was SO worth it. #lovereigns

17. You matter. Anything contrary to that idea is a lie.

It's Sunday Another day to love Happy Sunday

There is nothing I would not do for those who are really my friends. I have no notion of loving people by halves, it is not my nature.

Jane Austen

march

Sunday Morning Ramblings: March 2015

1. Do you realize there are people playing God? Really try not to be one of them. And especially do NOT follow those people. #sinklikeastone

2. Love is not hard. It's smooth. However, you might have to let go of your pride. That part is not smooth. #lovesoftly

3. If you lost something very precious, would you go look for it? Don't lose yourself. Way too precious. #weALLneedYOU

4. Within love is freedom and true faith. All these folks who say they have faith and then don't love, come up empty. #emptyhearts #emptypockets

5. I never want to hold onto an idea so tightly that I bleed. #openhearts

6. I fail miserably in all the above mentioned, at times. #keeponlovin

7. In fact, in my imagination I am a failure. I'm also a blooming success. #rightmindclub

8. I'm more present than ever. Which makes me more pleasant. #churchwasNOTtheplaceforme

9. So, there are gay men. There are transgendered folks. There are lesbians. There are hetero people. Whatever you are don't make it seem like YOU are the ONLY group. You're not. #beBRAVEandcrossthedivide #weareinthisthingTOGETHER

10. Years ago a few family members mocked and spoke hateful things about me. It was caught on video tape (no joke). I decided then that my artsy ways were not for the masses. So I stopped attending family functions. Many spoke negatively about me. And they still do. Some younger family members were told lies about me. Now they're adults. I don't have many family relations. I've had to make my own family. Thank goodness I have the most beautiful human beings in my life. It's hard. Really hard. However, it has taught me one of the greatest lessons about people who may appear different on the outside and the fear that is stirred up by this. We have a choice how we respond. #loveisTHEanswer

11. Hate is a waste. Hate is waste. Waste is an unusable byproduct. Waste can be hazardous. #dontWASTEhating

12. I used to work for a bra manufacturer in a little town in New Jersey. This company also helped women with breast prosthetics. One day a transgendered man came in to get fitted for a bra and prostheses. I was young. And alone. And afraid. The boutique I worked in was on the street. I phoned the owner and asked her to come in. She did. In the most loving way I watched her as she measured this man's chest, fitted him with a bra, gently handling the prosthetics. He was kind. And sad. He left the shop and remained a loyal customer for years after that. My 22yo self

asked her how she could do that so lovingly. She explained that we are all human beings. To treat one any differently than you'd want to be treated goes against nature. #Irestmycase #hugelesson

13. If you don't know how to love people who are different than you, don't worry about it. Until someone comes into your life who IS different, you really have no way to practice. However, if you are certain that you're life and lifestyle is the ONLY way, there will be people, who are different, coming in droves. #practicemakesperfect

14. Everything I write here is for myself, too. #lifelearner

15. It seems as though the Universe is rigged in our favor. This does not mean LIFE is a dream. #lessons #wisdom

16. Yesterday, I was floating. I spent the afternoon with friends as we perused the art scene in our city. Chatting with artists, gazing and losing myself in their works, learning and growing as a friend, laughing til my tummy ached. All for a good cause. LIFE. #donotforgettolivewhileyouarehere

17. I heard spring is coming soon. #toatheaternearyou

It's Sunday. Another day to love. Happy Sunday

Sunday Morning Ramblings: March 2015

1. When I was in my late 20's I was hired as a mascot for Wolfe Communications. Wolfie. A very tall purple wolf. I paraded around malls and events. Children hugged me. Adults gave me

"high fives." It was a very secret happening; living inside a large furry suit peering through a mesh barrier carrying a huge happy wolf head while dragging Clydsedale sized feet through a parade making sure not to trip over my tail. I loved every bit of it. #weirdjobs

2. What is beauty? I just viewed a video of a group of older Jewish folks explaining a few Yiddish words. These people are so beautiful. My grandma was beautiful. I used to stare at her face while she spoke. Diving into each crevice in her skin as a road map taking me to the most exotic destination. I couldn't get enough of her knowledge, her love. At some point, someone demands that we compare "this beauty" against "that beauty." And we listen. As minutes become hours then days, weeks, years we find ourselves amidst the battle of beauty. #thebeautyisYOU #nomorefighting

3. Be good. It's really not that difficult. #unlessyouareselfish

4. Greed is ugly. #takingmorethanyougive

5. Mocking is not to be tolerated. #thebruntofmanyhurtfuljokes

6. I love kindness. It's gentle and sweet. And clean.

7. I'm feeling a bit caged lately. This is NOT good. #winterisSOover

8. I get answers to some really perplexing and deep questions while I sleep. Last night I was given wisdom regarding a situation that happened between me and one of my closest friends from high school. Mind blower. #payattention

9. Possession of another person is really gross. It can happen slowly over time. Be careful. It can happen between friends, too. Take care with this one. #jealousy

10. Having an appreciation for someone on a deep level is a rich awareness. It connects us with ourselves, truly. Worshipping someone, on the other hand, is just plain odd. #peopleFINDyourPLACE

11. There's a guy in my kitchen making fresh coffee right now. #beansinthegrinder

12. My sons are so independent. Really. 14 and 11 yo. It's as though time is whizzing by and I'm standing still holding my breath. Then they say, "Mom, can you get me something to drink?" Then I breathe again. #watchingthemgrow #privilegedmomma

13. I've been in my current job for close to 15 years. It's the longest, richest work I have ever done. #Iamfreakinexhausted #cannotwaittoretire

14. The news is not news. It's olds. It's uglies. It's hurt-fulls. It's pains. It's lies. It's torments. It's dirties. It's means. It's nothings. #becarefulwhatyoufollow #youmaybecomeIT

It's Sunday. Another day to love. Happy Sunday

Tis better to have loved and lost than never to have loved at all.

Alfred Lord Tennyson

April

Sunday Morning Ramblings: April 2015

1. 14+ years. $$$$$$$ to a lie. Oh and let's not forget the pockets that we padded and the facials and vacations we paid for....I'll get over this at some point, hopefully. Oh and a family of people making an entire congregation feel like a piece of dirt then wonderful then a piece of crap then amazing then a piece of... you get the picture. #itscalledachurch #theytakefromwidowstoo #theytakefromthepoor

2. Be careful what you believe in. It could be a Ponzi wolf in sheep's clothing.

3. I'm moving on. Truly.

4. I'll take my imperfections over theirs any day.

5. Hope believes all things. And then the blind shall see, the lame shall walk, etc. I'm beginning to believe that the book called the Bible is really more of a warning than anything else. "Stay away from the thieves."

6. This thing is big. And very, very sad.

It's Sunday. Another day to love. Happy Sunday.

And the day came when the risk to remain tight in a bud was
more painful than the risk it took to blossom.

Anais Nin

may

Sunday Morning Ramblings: May 2015

1. Peace is truly everything it claims to be.

2. My sons came to teach me.

3. Don't be confused. Those folks who are bristly on the outside are truly tender meat on the inside. #findtheirsoftspot And those who are outwardly tender are a lot tougher than one might think.

4. Laying down your life for a friend shouldn't mean you die. I don't think a true friend would ask that of you. It's kinda mean.

5. Started my day with a shot of Chlorophyll. #green

6. My husband bought me an unexpected gift the other night at an art show we attended. I LOVE it. He also installed really cool LIGHTS IN OUR NEW AND IMPROVED SWANKY BUTLER'S PANTRY!!!!!!!!!!!!!!!!!!!!!!!!!!!!!!!!! *a girl's heart is where IT is #lowmaintenance

7. Lemon water is changing our lives. #goodbyeacidreflux

8. While falling asleep the other night I was thinking about how, now that the boys are older, I don't get woken up in the middle

of the night anymore and how I'm loving my new bedtime routine and all the glory that comes with sleeping and yada yada yada yodel....whooooohoooooo....and then, "MOM!!!!!!!!!!!!! MY EAR!!!!!!!!!!!!!!!!!!!!!! Yep. #screamingearinfection #springfever #nosleep #offtothedocs #livingonhoneythisspring #Ihadbandrehearsalintheafternoonandfelthungover #wentobedat8oclock #IreallydoLOVEmylife

9. I married a really cool guy. #saiditbefore #Iwillsayitagain

10. That cult community (aka: *a church*) that we are no longer a part of is still demanding money from widows and the poor. #sosad #tryingonforgiveness

11. We gave 15 years to that place ^ and its people and so much money and time. My soul was exhausted. I had to get that out. I had to type that and see it in print. Now, I'm crying. Not sure if the tears are from the loss, the hope that never amounted to anything, the plundering that these people are getting away with, the embarrassment of believing in a loving community where our sons could have a semblance of family, or my own stupidity and weakness. I'm sure it's a blend of it all. A Ponzi scheme where no one is going to be held accountable, no one is going to prison...and the worst, for me, no one is going to apologize and admit what they are doing is wrong. #havetogetoverit #takersultimatelyreceivenothing

12. We have lost a lot ^ time, money, energy, health. But, what is truly a loss when INTEGRITY stands firm and HONESTY and BRAVERY hold humanity's sword and LOVING HEARTS still manage to beat and the GIFT GIVER still gives? #cannottakeLOVEfromme

13. While the caged bird may still sing, have you seen how beautiful a free bird soars? #soaring

14. No one can fix your problems. But it never hurts to ask for help, if you need it.

15. It appears that every lesson in life is multi-layered.

16. Trust yourself. #itllbeOK

It's Sunday. Another day to love. Happy Sunday.

Sunday Morning Ramblings: May 2015

1. Labels...right at the nape of our necks causing jerky head movements and twists and red rashes. An annoyance all the livelong day. I tear those crusty labels out of my shirts. And the person who decided to print the label instead is a kind human. Thank you. But can we remove all the labels? I'd like to. Maybe only keep the ones that inform us: what's in our food or medication or supplements or other products for consumption or

our use. Yes. Keep those. But the other labels that make us all twisted and jerky and red...those...I'd like to banish those. #metaphordrip #keepyourheartsopen

2. I've got a story. It's long. It's being expressed in song. This means, I'll be singing it. Soon. #songandstory

3. You've got a story, too. If you feel moved to share it, I hope you do, using whatever process or medium or method you can. It's important. I'd like to hear it. #perfectstars

4. I do not care what others think of me. However, I do care what I think of myself. #canyoulivewiththat

5. I felt Saturday yesterday. You know Saturday? That gorgeous moment in time when you're free in the warm air, nothing holding onto you, but a gentle blend of all the goodness and freedom and freewill that the Universe could offer. Right there, in that moment, just for you. #freefromthetrappings

6. Deciding to be present means we all get to share our authenticity with each other. #beautifulpeople #Ilovepeople

7. My sons are musicians. For real. #OMG

It's Sunday Another day to love Happy Sunday

Sunday Morning Ramblings: May 2015

1. When a shift happens, let go and let it happen. Everything will be alright. And if in that shift friendships change or dissolve or you become more aware of a new truth, whatever you do, DO NOT resist. Being stuck is sticky business. #flypaperLIFEisNOTliving

2. I have some new friends. And. I love them.

3. I also have some of the same friends that I've had for a long time. And. I love them.

4. There was a girl party at my house yesterday. And. I love them. #girlparties #weddings

5. Our little dog...almost died...a few years ago. Chased a woodchuck underneath our shed. Got her collar stuck in a tree root. Hottest summer in our history in upstate New York. We couldn't find her. For 6 days. Then we found her. Then EC dug her out. Our neighbor gave her a sip of water. Then she was alive. And well.

6. Two weeks ago that same little dog almost died. Paralyzed from her midsection down. Day after day listening to her crying and whimpering in pain. On meds. Nothing to do for her. Carrying her out to do her business. Feeding her with a dropper. Loving her up. Saying goodbye. Holding her, sharing stories. Then, she lifted her head. Then she stood up. Then she walked Then she managed the stairs. Then she went outside. And fell over. Then we carried her. Then she stood up.

Then she took a few steps. Then she wagged her tail. Then she started barking. Then she went for a walk. Then she was alive. And well.

7. We realized our little dog is a cat.

8. Learn some lessons from the creatures. They got it going on, man. #findthosewhowillholdyouwhenyoufallover

9. I am not a Type A personality. #relief

10. Take some chances with your life. Even a deep breath. It'll change everything. #oxygendeficit=nolife

11. Don't look back. Unless you've dropped something you might need. #forwardismoving

12. I want to say something about a dear, dear friend that has offered his GIANT LOVE to our family in a way that makes this MUSH OF A HUMAN BEING ever so grateful our paths crossed. The other day while I was LOST this same friend saw me. And I followed him down the road. And IT, yes IT has made ALL the difference. #forksintheroad #followLOVE #drippingmetaphors

13. We do not do anything alone. #deepbonds #togetherness

14. EC painted our entryway. Whoop! We are on a roll #whenONEthingchangesEVERYTHINGchanges

15. I painted the window boxes. #colorFULLliving

It's Sunday. Another day to love. Happy Sunday

Sunday Morning Ramblings: May 2015

1. Life is a series of loves. Our next thought might be...and a series of losses. This is true. We really do lose things; thoughts, stuff, people, our beloved animal friends. In the mix, is this thing called LOVE that remains. It is what gets us to DO or BE anything in this life. It's what moves us along. It's how we got started and landed on this big blue marble. I've heard that LOVE is forever. I'll get back to you on that one. However, true love is a constant. Yesterday morning we said goodbye to our sweet seemingly live-forever doggie. We held her and cried and let her go. And our hearts broke. Twelve years with us without an end in sight...is how we live. My hope is that we ALL choose to LIVE without an end in sight.

2. There is an immeasurable volume of tears flowing today. #weLOVEyouKylieGirl

3. If you'd like to know what I'll be doing after I pen this post: caring for my sons, rubbing their backs, holding them, feeding them nutritious food, letting them watch ALL the movies they want, printing out photos of our Kylie for their walls, sharing stories about our sweet fur baby, and crying...

4. Here's the story of how our lives became blended with one of the cutest creatures on the earth. Our friend told us of a dog that was found in the city. She was keeping all the kitties away from a neighbor's home, barking her head OFF as these felines tried to make their way to the back porch and their wee kitty door. Kylie was having nothing to do with it. Oh, she didn't live in that

house. She just didn't care for cats. She was lost. For weeks. The kind folks kept her in the house, and placed all their kitties upstairs, in a spare room. Flyers were posted all over the neighborhood, phone calls were made. No one claimed her. So. Our friend called us up and told us about this creature. At that time our oldest son was 4yo and our youngest, was 1yo. I was stressed to the max and NO WAY GETTING A DOG TO TAKE CARE OF, TOO! WHAT, ARE YOU KIDDING? In walks this half-grown-out-perm furred adorable creature with a feather duster for a tail. EC and I and our sons are sitting in the living room. The kind folks put her on the floor and she makes a beeline for me, right up into my lap. #endofstory

5. I'm a pushover.

6. Losing her furriness stirs up memories of all our losses. And all our loves.

7. Tender hearts live at this address. And as my 11 yo says, "I need to cry right now and feel ALL of this, so that I don't forget her." #foreverfriends

8. We listened to the Beatles on the way to the animal hospital yesterday. "And when all the brokenhearted people living in the world agree, there will be an answer, let it be."

9. Pain is soft and deep.

10. I will never regret all the love that I give.

11. And I will never apologize or be ashamed of it either.

It's Sunday. Another day to love. Happy Sunday.

To be yourself in a world that is constantly trying to make you something else is the greatest accomplishment.

Ralph Waldo Emerson

June

Sunday Morning Ramblings: June 2015

1. I know it's not morning. However, it is morning somewhere. #timezonefree

2. I'm processing my experience from Friday night. Bear with me #deeplytouched #firstGIG

3. This morning the "right" thing for all four of us to do was go eat breakfast at one of the other Coffee Connection locations in our city. This one is down the road from our house. They weren't open. So we went to the location where I sang on Friday evening. This time I ATE there. YOU REALLY NEED TO EAT THERE! #whenIsayTHEBESTFOODImeanit #fooddesigners #healthyhomecooked #scrumptious

4. There is a dog at my feet...pretty much everywhere I am in the house or outside. I like it. #newpuppy #IamtheMomma #hisnameisSergeant

5. I miss my far away friends...so much I could cry. #memories #closeness

6. I'm gearing up to do a Ted Talk or something like this. Don't have any clue about the details. But I can see myself wearing the headset mic and walking and talking across the stage. You know what I'm talking about intuitive friends.

7. I posted #6. I didn't delete it. The Universe reassured me it was gonna be alright. #jumpinglikeinsideabouncyhouse #butverycalminside (This became a reality 2019) Wow!

8. I dropped Fear from the end of my name. And added StarBright. Kolein Velvette Evelyn Ann StarBright Carlson. #stardust

9. Who's joining me?

10. I'm no longer kidding. I have found too many of my lost pearls. #freetofindpearls #yourpearlsareYOURS

11. I'm crying now. #tearstreamer

12. There are several folks I know who are trapped inside a fear based religion. I want you to know, in case you are taking a chance and reading this today, I'm holding your pearls, keeping them warm with the love from my heart. However, you have to find them yourself. #itisNOTeasy #ItisFREEDOM

13. We need each other. #forever

14. I love my new life. My real, new life. #juststartedtoday #juststartedthismoment

15. Yoga.

It's Sunday. Another day to love. Happy Sunday.

Sunday Morning Ramblings: June 2015

1. This has been a week. Epic.

2. The Supreme Court, the highest court in the land, deemed marriage equality, well, equal. It's a HUGE step. HUGE. We ALL feel that, no matter what we, individually or personally or as a group, think about it. If I could suggest one thing to everyone...think about it, not merely with your brains or your belief systems or your religions and your holy books or the political bias you engage in or what you've been taught or how you are afraid...take a moment to figuratively (or literally, if you know someone who happens to be gay, lesbian, bi-sexual, transgendered) look in the eyes of that person, sense their spirit...their true essence and then...then...then...take a deep breath...let it out and go live your life with love. #anythingelseisFEAR

3. My father loved watching All In The Family back in the 70's. My father is a gentle-man. Yet I'd see his kind self morph into a tougher radical. He was agreeing with Archie's bigotry. I became appalled. These were the ONLY subject matters of our disagreements. I'd sit with him and watch the show and the outcome, which showed Archie soften and come around to a deeper understanding of humanity and let go of his grumbly-spirited, limited thinking (ok that's a stretch, but that was the point). This character never became truly enlightened as each week there'd be another episode of his dealing with race, cultures, gender, etc. Hence the show. However, the lessons learned were wonderful. Archie was a softy. I actually grew to like his character. He was being honest with the information he was tightly holding onto about people and groups, etc. But life

would throw him a curve ball. He'd eventually be needing the help of the black man, the liberal, or gasp...the hippie, his eyes being opened to humanity, no matter the differences. I learned a lot about my dad, too. His limited view was askew. He was still a loving man who had been taught certain beliefs. It became my "job" to help Dad see. When I told him that a very close friend, whom he adored, was gay he was in complete denial for years. But then told me, he loved the man. He didn't understand but he loved him just the same. #lovewins #lovethebigottoo

4. Fear is tricky. It tells us to STAY when it is alright to MOVE-FORWARD.

5. "No, I don't see a color. I see skin. I see a person." My best friend's older sister didn't believe me. Until, one day, many years later, she did. #theworldisBlacktheworldisWhite #seetheLIGHT

6. This is me. Right here. Standing on the roof top, shouting to everyone down below. I love people...you can count on ME, Kolein Velvette Carlson to LOVE you...NO MATTER WHAT. #Igottadosomething #everyoneDOsomething ##loveMATTERS

7. I have a dream...that one day, perhaps today, we wake up and believe that LOVE is the answer, the ONLY answer. EVER. #itisEASY

8. If in your heart you have tension, you do not have love. If in your mind, there is confusion, you do not have love. If in your spirit you are gray, you do not have love. #askforhelp #cryoutforhelp

9. Examine yourself. #openmind #openheart

10. Systems are broken. Families are broken. Religions are broken. Love is still the answer. #itsSObigyoucanFINDitANYWHERE #remembertolook #itsInYOU

11. Evolve a little today. It's ok if we're scared. We can be afraid together. Take my hand. Walk this way.

12. Together...we GROW to see the light.

It's Sunday. Another day to love. Happy Sunday.

Sunday Morning Ramblings: June 2015 Father's Day

(To my distant father who is always in my heart, who will never be on FB to see this, who lives in fear of his past, who is trying to make a little life for himself, who will be 83 this August, who loves God, who used to hide in the corner shaking when he was a kid, who is an artist of epic proportions, whose singing voice would make you weep, whose wood working art is still jaw dropping, who my sons will most likely never really get to know, who my husband adores, and whose daughter cries about wishing life and choices and people were different and kinder so that YOU, Dad, Daddy, Poppy could be in our lives and we could enjoy you for a few more days because we ALL LOVE YOU.)

1. Dad, what you don't know is that I don't care about your mistakes.

2. As a parent now myself, I certainly do not want my children to care about mine.

3. I love you anyway.

4. I hope my children love me anyway.

5. Dad, you gave me all that you were, even the broken bits and they made me a tender human being.

6. Tenderness is my favorite part of myself.

7. Your artistry made, and makes, me dream vividly. It is why I am an artist.

8. I forgive you for only buying me Loretta Lynn, Patsy Cline and Glen Campbell albums when I was a teenager.

9. I always set out to make you proud, since that time I wore a bowl of spaghetti on my head when I wasn't yet 2 years old and even today at 51.

10. That little dark black time in my life? Awe, it was nothing. I was trying out the F word.

11. I am your little girl, forever.

12. Thank you for loving all my friends when we were younger. They still ask about you and LOVE you too.

13. My favorite story about me that you told umpteen times..."and I held you for the first time and thought, Oh I'm gonna love her and spoil her"...I'd love to hear it again.

14. I love how we can get into a really rich conversation and start weeping together and then burst out laughing.

15. I think in a past life we were BEST FRIENDS.

16. I miss you.

17. I will always love you no matter what. However, not seeing you is really a challenge to understand. I love you anyway.

Happy Father's Day to those men who really want to be everything for their families but life has gotten in the way of their trying and caused a great divide. May love be the unifying force that heals this separation.

It's Sunday. Another day to love. Happy Sunday.

Sunday Morning Ramblings: June 2015

1. I think mean people get away with a lot more than they should. #BeNice #itwillnothurtyou

2. I listened to someone's ego speak recently. It was as though I could see his future unfolding right before my eyes. #religiontrap #egowantsitALL

3. It's about time for me to sit near some water and stay there for hours or days...alone. #gottathink

4. The puppy? He's doing great. He's a maniac. Until he's not. Then he sits at our feet or sprawls out in the family room. He's learning about us. He talks. Liza, our girl, doesn't talk much.

She's a graceful lady. Sergeant, is a bit sloppy. I don't do sloppy.
So we'll be training him to be more of a gentleman. I do like it
that he speaks to me when he wants something.
#goodGODwegottanotherDOG

5. Being a home educator is one of the highest privileges EVER.
#adayinthelife

6. My sons have such wisdom and bravery.
#deepintheSOULkind

7. We haven't been in a church building since our awakening.
Recently, we were for a special ceremony. Amazing how when
the heart speaks you are warm and in the moment with the
speaker and as soon as the spirit of that speaker changes to the
dark side, it's time to walk out. #deeperawareness
#donotgivecreditwhereNONEisdue

8. The heart of people is the true connection. What is everybody
so afraid of? #taughtofear

9. There are many robot people in church buildings,
programmed to think and behave in a particular way. It makes
me sad. As though our lovely selves are not good enough to be
who we truly are. #fear #trustwithinourselves

10. I love kindness; gentle kindness. #iamlearningtobekinder

11. The other day, in a public place, I witnessed a depth of fear
from someone I used to know from *that place*. #deepdeepsadness
#whoa

12. Folks are told to shun us. When the reality is they are being trained to shun their TRUE selves. #sosad #thereisabetterway #beingawake #iusedtobeasleepwithONEeyeOPEN

13. Johnny Cash always wore black. I read one time, until there was peace in the world, he wasn't going to wear any other *color*. I'm doing something like this, in my mind and heart. Until folks are free, and I realize that's a giant hope, I will continue to LOVE and not stop. #write #sing

14. I've got some gardening to do today - one with the earth and sky. And hopefully this time I can manage to plant without the puppy digging everything up. #hethoughtIwasplayingagame #funny #notfunny

It's Sunday. Another day to love. Happy Sunday

You don't have a soul. You are a soul. You have a body.

CS Lewis

July

Sunday Morning Ramblings: July 2015

1. I meditate in the grocery store. No really, I do. It's easy. A few deep belly breaths in the produce section. Grab a melon. Give it a squeeze. Make eye contact with the grocer or a customer, smile sweetly. Move onto the next section, methodically. Pick up a new item that I've never tried before. Read the ingredients. A few more deep breaths. Move on. By the time I'm finished and at the checkout I feel like I can get through this shopping experience. I think I have onset ADD, whenever I go into a store with fragrances and sounds and lighting! Yikes! Being present is the name of the game, baby.

2. I love happy beginnings. I love happy middles. I love happy endings that are actually beginnings. So. I love never ending happies. #love #lookforit

3. Finding a parking spot directly in front of Archimage on Monroe Avenue is what I refer to as a "little lucky." I used to survive on those "little luckies" all along the way. I've graduated now. I'm going for the BIG luckies now.

4. I've got roots. #intheground #onmyhead

5. Living in the same community as the other community we used to know is quite alarming and subtly freeing. Being publicly shunned is starting to get a bit funny, while remaining deeply sad. #gratefulbeyondwords #theyareAFRAIDofthemenontheplatform #ugliness #fear

6. Get to know your heart. Whatever we do in this life, let's at least do that. And once you've introduced yourself to that beating, beautiful heart, sit down with it, thank it, talk to it, but most of all...listen to it. #ithasyourBESTinterest

7. The further we get away from the "swinging Bible" the closer we are to the truth. It is a LOVELY DAY. #meanpeopleareNOTnice

8. Are you spending time on your higher loves or your lower loves? This question was just asked of me. I know the answer. So now I think I'll make a shift. #thankfulfortheUniverseanditspeople #choices

It's Sunday. Another day to love. Happy Sunday

Sunday Morning Ramblings: July 2015

1. Warning: Heart on Sleeve Day

2. You've been warned.

3. I have so much emotional scar tissue. I wonder, this morning, how many have been scarred by me.

4. My brokenness can bring on epiphanies. #socanyours

5. Moving-on usually means we are dragging that bag with us. Moving-through can mean we decide just what we're taking with us on our journey and what gets composted into, hopefully, good, rich soil. #digdeep

6. I have two huge forgivenesses to get through. One has to do with a family. I'll call them the Ponzi's and the other has to do with a memory of a hurt that keeps popping up. I tried to move on from the latter one but find I'm dragging that bag...still.

7. The Ponzis? Being duped allows for some fabulous self-examination, ultimately becoming self-actualization. What I've come up with so far? I really love myself. Finally.

8. Love yourself. It's OK. Go ahead. Try it. Even just a little at a time. #begood

9. I love the man my husband is. Not in a showy, wifey kind of way. But when I "got divine word" to leave that building we gave so much of our lives to, and I had to communicate that to EC, I truly thought he would divorce me. I wasn't upset for all the obvious reasons. I was upset because I wouldn't get to hang out with him and talk with him for hours and enjoy his company because I really, really LIKE him. So thinking we'd divorce, I thought, "Oh well. I knew him for 20 years." And then...he was "getting a divine word" too and guess what PEOPLE? We're still married!!!!!!!!! And guess what else??? We used to live in the most tied up, messed up FEAR based place EVER. It's in our city. It's awful. We wouldn't have gotten divorced. His coolness

would have chatted with my coolness and everything would have been...COOL. That's LOVE.

10. I have no idea why I just typed number 9.

11. These are ramblings.

12. My brother got married yesterday...to my sister-in-law. Toss hearts everywhere! They held a sign that said, "Never say never." #olderwise #heissogoodforher #iamhappy #iwanttoliveinVAnow

13. Church isn't a building, in case you believe in that malarkey. No disrespect to the Malarkeys.

14. I've finally gotten my spirituality back. The robbers got my money but they didn't get my soul. #phew

15. I don't hate the Ponzis. Not one bit. #hopingtheywakeup

16. Moving through....getting to some good, rich soil. Thank...me, God, Universe, Daisies, Stars...no one really knows. #letsbeHONEST

It's Sunday. Another day to love. Happy Sunday.

The best and most beautiful things in the world cannot be seen or even touched - they must be felt with the heart.

Helen Keller

August

Sunday Morning Ramblings: August 2015

1. We can be the anchor. We can be the boat. We can be the paddle. What I don't care to be?...the raging waters.

2. Peace is a good thing. #placidwaters

3. Yesterday, all day long, I shared love and laughter, hard work and fun, food and beverage, song and music with some crazy wild amazing gorgeous folks...who live on my street, in my neighborhood and in my city. I love them. #party #gathering #ourvillage

4. So, what is it that we deny? (fatty foods? the truth? love? ourselves? others? a good yoga stretch? deep conversation? hmmm?)

5. After the wildness and joy of a big party yesterday I'm feeling reflective, grateful, achy, bloated, satisfied, reclusive. #goodtimes

6. "Time will tell." We've all heard, or perhaps, said this at some point. It's true sometimes. However, in the moment, this one right here, there is an amazing story if we can just hang out for a bit. #slowdown #stoprushing

7. We are not the same person. #wildflowers #allofus #inthesamefield

8. Sometimes I am the sky.

9. We will not be traveling out west this summer. Time told me why. It's all good. Even though I will miss seeing our fabulous friends in Washington and Oregon and meeting our "new" nephew, Sean...time has assured me "it isn't the time." So. We'll be enjoying the east coast, somewhere.

10. These are ramblings.

11. She shed, she shed...by the sea shore? Or even the back yard. #needspacetocreate #basementstudio #chinup

12. Sergeant, our Dutch shepherd, now 8 months old, has become such a quirky, funny, loving member of our family. It makes my heart sing! #hetalkstous #heLOVESoursweetangeldogLIZA

13. I love to give.

14. I'm not looking at my TO DO list today. At all.

15. I have the absolute best people in my life. All of them. I trust them. I love them. They care about me, EC and the boys. We help each other in a sweet kind natural way. And not one of them has demanded I clean their bathroom with a Q-tip or pick up the minutest brown pieces of tree debris from their property or told me my spirit wasn't right if I disagreed with them or gave me a disgusted look for dressing different than they do or for cutting my hair or wearing makeup or earrings or living freakin' life doing what we mere mortals do. It's quite refreshing to be in this world with the real people. #phew #sweetrelief #SOHAPPYIdidNOTdrinkthekoolaid #Ipreferwater

16. Stepping out. #ImakemyselfLAUGH

It's Sunday Another day to love. Happy Sunday

Sunday Morning Ramblings: August 2015

1. I cannot be everything. However, I can be me. #simple

2. I woke up yesterday. Again. As in, had an awakening. I was stressing all about my art and my music and my writing and fitting everything in and school approaching and cleaning the cobwebs in my house and reorganizing the studio downstairs and never getting to painting my kitchen cupboards for the 3rd summer in a row and then it hit me. Who am I? My answer came in the sweetest, most profound delicate whisper..."You are a mother, first." #lifesaving #peace

3. Now that voice didn't say "you are only a mother" or "you're nothing else" it simply reminded me where my priorities are and the peace, the peace is so gorgeous I could cry right now.

4. I love being a mother. #latebloomer

5. I told my oldest about this happening. Seeing his face, his expression...the gentle bend of his head toward the table as I spoke...the way he looked down...the tender smile he gave me when his eyes met mine...nothing could compare to that moment...to that gift in time. #gifts #love

6. Waking is hard to do. #hittingsnoozeisNOTtheanswer

7. I love to laugh. Did I ever mention that? Oh my. #fromtheBELLY

8. I'm not a group. I'm a person. I don't believe in groups. Groups single handedly omit relationship with individuals. I'm much better suited to be in relationship WITH people, one on one. Maybe because I'm many people loosely wrapped up into this one person, me. And. Add anymore to that and it's crowded. Or I get LOST, or someone else does. And that can make us feel lonely - within the group. Maybe because a group identity opens up pandora's box for judgment, or generalizations. I can't stand that. Also, I can't identify with a group. I'm too much me. There's so much beauty in the individual, in the relationship, in the potential of the single, one-on-one experience. Some say there is power in the group. Perhaps a force. But it takes real bravery to stand apart from that and examine who we are. #whereisyouridentity

9. These are ramblings. #hadmycoffeealready

10. Let yourself be today. Just a little. Stop nagging, poking, jabbing. You're really pretty special. #giveitathought

11. Perimenopause is so silly.

12. Ramblings!!!!

13. I cleaned a closet yesterday. Yep. One closet. I should get a reward or something. Don't ya think?

14. Yesterday I met a friend at BN on a spontaneous, "Hey ya wanna go to BN?" Five hours later I was back at home. #bookstoreLOVE

15. I'm happy right now. Like chemistry happy. You know the difference, right? #notondrugs #seretoninisUP #hangingatabookstoreHIGH

It's Sunday. Another day to love. Happy Sunday.

Sunday Morning Ramblings: August 2015

1. I like good people. The really good people. The people who are far and few...but the good find the good. They know each other immediately. They recognize their spirits at first glance. I like those people the best in all the world. #true

2. We received a thank you note in the mail the other day. It was from a young man we know. He acknowledged that our families have been through a lot together. And then he said it's good to know he can "always depend on us", that "we have each other." #truefriends #warmheart

3. My bitterness is fermenting into a gorgeous and useful compost. #realgrowth

4. I fell in love again. #umpteenthtime #husband #braveman

5. Mocking people may be a temporary way to feel like a giant among a crowd, but ultimately it is the quickest, most slippery way to loneliness. #becareful

6. I think therefore, I think. I am, because I am. #profundity

7. If you have a free moment to think for yourself...

8. I am not a category. I don't think of any of you as a category. #falseintimacy #highwayrobbery #stealingbeauty #ulitmatefear

9. I love my bike, like for real. Love it. #turquiose #giftfrommyguy

10. These are ramblings.

11. I miss my dad. #daughter #care #donotcareaboutmistakes

12. I wish the world were more perfectly in love with one another. #lovesomebodynewtoday

13. Don't buy into the language of "the separators" - those are the forces working against the gorgeous rhythm of life and living. #theyarethieves #media #bullies

14. This week we received four thank you notes in the US Mail. #thereisHOPEPEOPLE

It's Sunday. Another day to love. Happy Sunday.

Sunday Morning Ramblings: August 2015

1. My guys were on a four day canoe/kayak trip this past week. They took the puppy. On a canoe. On a lake. In the mountains. In a tent. #happycampers

2. Amazing how much time is in the day. Right? 24 glorious hours to do stuff and say stuff, sleep, go places, meet friends, stretch a body, watch a movie, quiet....oh lawd, the quiet. #Ilivedthose24hourslikenobodysbusiness #four24hoursinarow #canIgetaHallelujah

3. I remarked to my oldest last night there was one thing I did NOT do while they were away. (something I did yesterday, the entire day). Stand in the kitchen. #really #laughterensued

4. Moms, has it ever dawned on you how much we stand in the kitchen?? Seriously. Seriously. #eats #lifetimesinthekitchen

5. I fell in the love while they were away. #paintbrush #canvas #time

6. I want to kiss Time. I want to thank Time. I wanted to give Time a big ole hug. #present

7. Then, I realized the summer is almost over. There's just a little crumb left of it. #pressingmyfingerintothatcrumb

8. Bike riding yesterday. #love #Iwanttoridemybicycle

9. Don't let go of who you are. Ever. Please. We ALL need YOU, the real you, the true YOU. If you've lost who you are...do whatever you are able to find yourself again. There will be a collective sigh of relief when you do, from everyone who truly LOVES you. And your world will be right again. And their world will be right again, too. #theREALyou

10. We are realizing that *the place* we left (thank God) and its distorted truth/philosophy is actually the opposite of everything

that is clearly true. Like for say... being LOST. When we were there, we were lost. I was always trying to find myself. It broke my heart. I cried a lot. A lot. I was born into the gorgeous possibility of creative living. And when I was there I was always trying to find myself. It was dreadful at times. It was inner turmoil. Don't let people tell you who you are. Only YOU can know that, or find that for yourself. #donotgiveupthesearch

11. Life has a way, even the disgusting painful stuff, of being an incredible teacher, not only for ourselves and our spirits, but for those around us. #lifelearner

12. Love. Always put love first. #leastamountofregrets

13. Let fear stand in your way and you become the greatest coward. #bebrave #whatisfaith

14. I love people, even the people who used to be in our lives. I still love all of them. I still hope for all of them. I still keep thinking that a few of them will "wake up" and our phone will ring with the deepest heartfelt apology. If that day ever happens, oh "what a day that will be." #mylifeisfilledwithhope

It's Sunday. Another day to love. Happy Sunday.

If you cannot be a poet, be the poem.

David Carradine

September

Sunday Morning Ramblings: September 2015

THE FALL
Is it all supposed to fall?
Neck skin carrying our beautiful heads
for a lifetime
Cheek flesh offering us a seat
in all the most important places
in our story
Upper arms cradling babies, and puppies
and groceries and books and boxes
with such precision, such strength
Inner thighs treating us to
bends and climbs, pushing us
along our personal trail
Tummy muscle that in its own right
bears a burden of forgiveness, stretching
twisting, its elasticity is kindness
And yet...we crumble when the mirror
beckons for a closer look
It's simply a gentle whisper
"You've changed."
That's all we hear in our eyes.
The smooth voice, if we lean in closer,
"Look what you've become."

Your smiles have lifted not only
your flesh but the spirits of countless
others
Those arms have embraced dear friends
and family with a never ending devotion
Your eyes have allowed tears to
awaken a truth
Those lips have sipped warm beverages
and lingered in delicate kisses forging
ahead new life, new beginnings
That neck has been a source of comfort
and warmth
Your waist, a steady hold for young
and old as they navigate terrain
Your mere presence, a gift
And through it all...this business called a life...
all this privilege called living...we delay our
spirit strength until gravity's truth
shouts aloud with echo force
We tremble to wake up
Our truths become self- evident
The jump, essential
The fall, a mandate
Without it
we simply die in our skin.

It's Sunday Another day to love Happy Sunday

Sunday, ehem, Monday, Morning Ramblings: September 2015

1. Getting burned is never good. Unless you're a marshmallow. #pokeastickinit #andburnit

2. The backyard is cleared out for the upcoming season of campfires, roasted weenies and fall shenanigans. #firepit #miniforest

3. Had another person nearly run away from me while shopping the other day. (I knew them really well from that past life experience.) Does anyone else find this odd? I wonder if that person does. #freetobewhat? #alltheBESTreligionsSHUN

4. Those experiences, stated in #3, are truly disheartening. I don't like them. I feel them deeply. #movingsoon

5. Stuffed peppers heal my soul. #yums

6. Some folks think outside the box. Some folks refuse to even see the box. Some folks pretend to be in the box, but are leaning over the edge peering out. Some folks jump out of the box. Some folks cut the box and throw it in the recycle pile. Some folks use the box to carry stuff to the curb. #boxes

7. I'm working through stuff all the livelong day. #carryingboxestothecurb

8. I was accepted to be in a local art show. #happy #excited #bettergetsewingandpainting #myoldneighborhood

9. *They* said "don't believe in yourself." Can you imagine? #deepsorrow

///

10. We can wake up to something new and beautiful...every...single...moment. #weareNOTwashedup

11. All roads are long...especially the roads that take us to the greatest destinations. #takingtheonelesstraveled

12. My first date with EC a million years ago, we went cross country skiing UP into the Adirondack mountains. He held my hand and believed in me. #needIsaymore

13. I know, I know, you've forgotten who you are. You're disconnected from your authenticity. You're trying like the dickens to find yourself. That journey can be exhausting. It can be most arduous. Remember to breathe and trust yourself. Please, please, trust yourself. And please...please...take a step... forward. And if you can, find someone to hold your hand. #Iwannaholdyourhand

14. Don't worship anyone. Please. It is a disconnect so deep inside the sinew and fibers of our being that once it has tied itself in...there may be no way to undo its strangulation on our soul. #please

15. Love, instead. There is freedom in love.

16. To place oneself above another means that we've never moved out of the mentality of master and servant, landowner and slave, Lord and peasant. Demeaning our value wastes precious lives. It's a choice, however. #modernslavetrade

17. Expressions are true. True expressions are. Are expressions true?

It's monday. Another day to love. Happy monday.

The person who follows the crowd will usually go no further than the crowd. The person who walks alone is likely to find himself in places no one has ever seen before.

Albert Einstein

October

Sunday Morning Ramblings: October 2015

1. I love young people. Really. I used to be one of them. And in some circles I still am one. When I walk into a store or down the street I remain forever, in my mind, a young person. And then a gray haired man smiles at me. Then I'm reminded I'm in my 50's. Nobody without gray hair looks at me now. When I was 'age young', if a gray hair looked at me he was *my grandpa* in the store. A "store grandpa." Now the gray haired guy who smiles is my "store boyfriend." Ok. This is NOT the point of this piece. At all. Gosh, you'd think I was subject to rambling. Back on track...young people. They've got it going on. For real. They have hopes, dreams...inspirations that get actualized like I've never witnessed before. With the computer age we receive this information all day, at times live streaming. Good for them. For real.

2. But girls and boys, here's the news flash: Stop giving your youth away! Stop kicking it down the street like an old crushed can! We've got to take back our lives, our experiences, our voices and our bloody hearts!

3. We've got life left...in our lives. Ok, so the body bends a little differently now. And we have wrinkles. Really? Like this is an issue. Our looks or lack of were an issue when we were young. Gotta get over this now. It's time. You really don't want to waste

a second on that anymore, do you? Those mirrors didn't convince you then. They aren't gonna do it now.

4. Let's talk about our bloody hearts. Bloody, as in they're still beating. Pumping blood. Perhaps that's stating the obvious. Take a moment. Think about this.

5. Bloody hearts. We, as age older people, have hearts that have been through it ALL. We are not reading a poem about life anymore. We have lived the freakin' poem, every line. We now write our own poems. And our own songs. Our age old pain is prolific in quantity, yes. Are you sitting down? Our age old pain is fertile, too, producing living organisms. You didn't know, did you? You didn't know that this half life that you've lived so far was actually made for producing life, living, creating, stories, happenings, wisdom, art, movement, joy, understanding, depth, care...

6. You are fertile. We need you. You need me. You have flowers AND seed. The conveyor belt is carrying so much of us to be shipped out PRIME, two-day FREE. Yet, some of us are sitting in the break room complaining.

7. So here's the gist...realize that you, yes you, the you right now is here for a purpose or maybe seven purposes or 20. Your story, your voice, your wrinkles, your baggage all carry a melody. There are ears and hearts sitting in some room in some town who need what you've got. Everyone is a star. Are you twinkling? Are you shooting across the sky? Or are you dim?

8. I believe in you. I believe in you because I need you to believe in me. You've got something so creative, so vulnerable that sets you apart from the others. Hello! That's why you're here. There's only one of you.

9. Dig deep and pay attention to that voice. What does it say? How does it speak? Have you found any pearls inside? Pearls of truth, pearls of wisdom? Keep digging. We have heard and read all of this before. It's being said in multiplicity perhaps, just perhaps, because we are all waiting on the edge of our seats...for you.

It's Sunday Another day to love. Happy Sunday

Sunday Morning Ramblings: October 2015

1. It is best to speak of what we really know to be true. It's not the easiest thing to do, always. #notwhatwethink #notwhatwehope #notwhatwehavebeentold #notwhatwebelieve #whatwetrulyKNOW

2. Bandwagons. Not for me. #donotaskmetojoin

3. What we believe isn't always good for everybody.

4. If we take anything by force, whether it is in words or actions, I don't believe it belongs to us. It's called stealing. #moments #beliefsystems

5. Strangers can be the kindest of all. They love in the moment. Then leave you in your moment. #warmth

6. Or they can be a comedy of errors.

7. When validation is no longer necessary, contentment and choice are yours. #betrulyfree #nolabels

8. If we follow people, beliefs, systems that are in the business of trying to change everyone...we may just find ourselves lost and very altered.

8.5. We are not all the same, nor are we supposed to be. We don't think the same, we don't come from the same story. I wish the world could truly see this and groups whether political or otherwise would stop trying to make everyone believe ONE way. #justbehuman #justbekind #itisprettysimple

8.75. If we criticize a group for not believing what we believe, how does that make us better? #nobandwagonsforme #freedomislove

9. I can't explain everything. I get asked a lot of deep questions. #motherofsons

10. If you love, then let that be who you are. If you don't, then don't harm anyone. Go softly. It'll be ok. #kindwords

11. Let Good be what we offer those around us. If you can't find that, then stay home. Or stay in your room. Or call someone who may have a bit of good to spare. Then come out. And be with the rest of us. #onlywayforhealing #onlywayforlovetohappen #speakingtomyself

12. I want to redesign my house. #sowhatelseisnew

13. Ramblings.

14. I also want to move. Somehow. Somewhere. Sometime. Some way. #choices

15. At the art festival, two weeks ago, I was exposed to all the elements. Heart. Painting. Creations. Inspiration. Cold. Wind. Rain. #Iamforeverchanged #hardwork #haveNOTcreatedablippinthingsincethen

16. Feeling stuck today. #nobodyneedstodoanything #Iappreciateit

17. I'm hankering for a creative time with friends and soup. #whowouldliketojoinme

18. I love sweaters, scarves, hats, gloves, boots and thick socks more than is humanly possible. #fall #winter

19. I have cooked more with apples in the last two weeks than I have in my entire lifetime. #cake #pie #sauces

20. My novels, while most of them remain in my head, are a running read throughout my day - not unlike a movie. I am the characters and setting. #hmm

21. Getting rid of all my clothes except for a few pieces. Starting ALL over. #refreshing

22. I love our dogs... #Liza #Serg

It's Sunday. Another day to love. Happy Sunday.

Do not look for healing at the feet of those who broke you.

anonymous

november

1. Look friends, *they* didn't ruin it ALL for us. *They* robbed us blind. For sure. But now we see. Isn't that cool? We SEE. As in open eyes and smiles and hearts and breathing.

2. No more grips around our throats or our bodies or our closets or our lives or our minds or the very construct of who we are, like the one that makes the flowers in the field all unique.

3. Sure we had hope. We take that with us. Don't leave it there. Don't give your hope away.

4. That gorgeous hope that had you waking up early on a Saturday handing out bags of peanuts with a loving heart.

5. That gorgeous hope that had you running around like a crazed chicken without a head for people who made you think they were actually helping "the world" along or helping you.

6. That gorgeous hope that made you believe in something supernatural and amazing and alive.

7. That gorgeous hope that laid your hand on someone's shoulder and prayed for THEIR gorgeous hope and help and healing and joy.

8. That gorgeous hope that carries us along on this journey that twists this way and that and takes our breath away and churns

giggles in our bellies and makes us dance on the tomorrows that come after yesterdays so bleak.

9. That gorgeous hope that doesn't believe in lack or that your light only shines if you've made the cut or that there are an elect FEW.

10. That gorgeous hope that believes ALL of us count, that we ALL matter and that taking from others is NOT what HOPE does...EVER.

11. HOPE. It's you. It's in you. In the fiber of your being.

12. It's what you're made of...a love so true...so real...that even when the wolves on this earth, mean arrogant people who live to take everything YOU are...whether made by a supreme being or a robust moment in time...while on this journey, YOUR journey, not theirs or their proclaimed masterful puppeteer's hand.

13. But YOUR journey trying to discover the REAL you, the REAL being, what you came for, is there a reason, what drives you, what impassions you, what holds your heart so delicately from the ravaging winds of man's arrogant mistakes.

14. What makes you the YOU that no one, not even a mean troubled man or an angry woman or a whole entire family or an organization that drove your passions for their own gain could EVER,
Ever,
EVer
take away

YOU, that gorgeous YOU
is still there holding
onto hope.

15. Don't throw that away.

It's Sunday. Another day to love. Happy Sunday.

Sunday Morning Ramblings: November 2015

1. America is not the government. I realize that statement is a bit
abrupt. Or maybe not. America is the people, right? America is
the people in your neighborhood, your coffee shop, your yoga
class, your doctor's office, your library. America is your circle or
square or trapezoid of influence, care, moments. America is me.
It's you. It's not leaning one way or the other. It's your heart
beat. It's your heart. It's your thought process. It's your mind or
body or soul that leans this way or that or simply stands up
straight for what is good and right in your sphere. America is
your hand picking up an empty coffee cup left for trash on the
side of your neighborhood street. And it's also the hand that
dangled and then flipped off the person who left the coffee cup
on the road for you to glare at in rage and do nothing about.

2. The political structure does not speak for me. I speak for me.
The manipulative powers that be do not know my name. They
have no influence on whether or not I vote one way or the other.
That is my choice. And to the best of who I am, I feel I chose
wisely. However, my choice is not based on what you think

about it or what is vomited from the back of the throats of the media. If you trust the news any longer...well...I feel for you.

3. So what do we trust? Ourselves. Get to know yourself. Get quiet for a few minutes and listen. Crap. I know it can be scarier than H-E-double hockey sticks. But seriously, if-IF-If you begin to listen, you not only hear your voice, you find it. The most precious part is, that voice is needed. If you are in my trapezoid of influence I need to hear it. If I am in yours, then my voice matters to you. However, your voice isn't mine. And mine isn't yours. That would be silly. That might be called the government, for crying out loud.

4. I do believe in collective voices, however. One is either the voice of love or the voice of fear. Two voices and all the different varieties that fall underneath these. That's it. I'm a lifelong psychology major. So far in my studies I have not come up with any other conclusions. This is actually really good news. Once you understand and hear your own voice and get in touch with its source, life becomes simple. Your understanding of it becomes clearer. Thus, your choices are easier to make - without drama or fanfare or rage or like a junkie trying to get a fix.

5. I love people. I don't mock them. Whatever they believe or however they express themselves or not or what they look like (really?) or whether their face turns beet red or they scare the begeebers out of me for lack of care or expression. It's that inner voice I listen to that demands I stay focused on what really matters. "Don't get distracted here, Kolein. There are things to do."

6. So, all this business about who will be president. Relax. It's gonna be ok. Just read some history. My 11yo is reading about every single president in our history, this year for school. He tells me about them. OK. I shudder. And yet, I'm amazed that we, as a country, are who we are...all our failures, all our faults, all our dis-ease, all our rage, all our troubles, all the lies and hypocrisy glaring us in the face...we remain a gorgeous, loving force in spite of it. That is because America is not the government. It's the people, you and me. We are the gorgeous, loving force.

7. Love is big. I don't care who wants to argue with this. It is. It is the one aspect of our humanity that remains intact. And that is why, people, I still have hope.

8. Fear is big, too. It ruins people, individually and collectively. Ultimately your decisions, daily, moment to moment come from either the F word or the L word. (that last bit really made me laugh)

9. My name is not PollyAnna. However, if we were in a crowd and you shouted that name, I'd probably turn toward your voice.

10. Rose-colored glasses are an excellent way to camouflage the wrinkles around the eyes of one who has seen and cried and blinked and winked and smiled and giggled during a beautiful and rich lifetime. Wear them if you need to...it'll do a body good.

11. I bought four new coffee mugs the other day. I love their size. I love their color. I love the pattern of leaves indented on

them. I love the feel of the mug in my hands as I take that first sip in the morning. Life is good.

12. We had to rebuild our four mailboxes at the end of our street. (well, Joe did.) (side note: Our town snow plow had destroyed them several times leaving them dangling and hanging on for dear life. America, the people, fixed the problem.) So, this meant that those over-sized teal bluish colored mailboxes I passed up last week at the Habitat for Humanity store got purchased and are now sitting out at the end of my driveway. Life is good.

13. It's a sunny fall morning here in upstate New York. Life is good.

14. I love my friends. All of them. They mean so much to me. I just wanna give 'em all a squeeze.

15. Souper Saturday will be happening here January, February and March. I'd love it if you'd join us. Savor a hot bowl of medicinal and spiritual goodness; throw in a hunk of homemade bread while sitting and chatting with lovely hearts. I'd say, life is good.

It's Sunday. Another day to love. Happy Sunday.

Sunday Morning Ramblings: November 2015

1. ...and so life goes on. It does because that's what LIFE is, living. I woke up this morning with peace. Why? I could say it's because I prayed last night. But honestly I don't know why I

have peace this morning. I'm under the weather, the boys are sick but we have music. And we have each other. And that is what matters...in our world. And that is what matters in your world, too. #turnonsomemusic

2. I considered the title "Sunday Mourning Ramblings."

3. I hope the arrogance of religion steps down from their high horses of "wisdom" and pauses for a moment to reflect and admit they do not have "the" answer.

3.5. I also hope the arrogance of politics steps down from their high horses of "wisdom" and pauses for a moment to reflect and admit they do not have "the" answer.

4. I have Empathic Order. (not to be confused with Empathic Disorder) I feel every deep emotion known to humanity. It used to be a punishment. Now, it is a great relief. #itisOKtofeel

5. I'm reminded over and over again (by one of my sons) that every time anyone points the finger at someone else, there are three fingers pointing back at them. What do I do with all this judgment? #decipheringmyfingers

6. Earlier this week my car was broken into. Also some homes were burgled while families slept - in a neighborhood nearby. There are thieves in this world. Takers. Of all shapes, sizes and flavors. That...is a fact.

7. If you're really pissed off this morning, or you were yesterday or the evening before....GOOD FOR YOU. Do something FANTASTIC with that energy. You will at the very least change

your inner world, perhaps your outer world or maybe even the ENTIRE WORLD. I've read of people doing that last bit before...you can Google it.

8. Be one of the helpers. Every. single. day.

9. My older son unknowingly shared some of his inner wisdom with me the other day (all kids do that). The Beatles are his favorite band for many reasons. While talking about their history, music, personalities, he mentioned John Lennon. I was trying to remember the name of the guy who changed our world on that dreadful day outside JL's apartment. My son stopped me: "Mom, don't say his name. Don't acknowledge him. That's what he wanted. He wanted to be famous alongside JL. I will never acknowledge a man who stole someone's life. I will never give him one ounce of attention. I choose to focus on life and in this case John Lennon's life and honor that any way I can." #Icried

10. A musician friend of ours passed away two weeks ago. He was the upright bass player in the band that EC has played in for many years. He played bass at our house, once a week for several years. He was a gentle man, a gentleman. We all loved him very much. #Bubba

11. Honor life. It's really a privilege.

12. I'm sure there are solutions, quite possibly several solutions to the world's problems. Cognitive dissonance is not one of them. Stubbornness is not one of them. And hate… sorry, it's not the answer either. #Ihavenoidea #whatistheanswer

13. I love coffee. Big huge cups of it.

14. These are ramblings.

15. Our puppy who is now the size of a small horse chewed my large ceramic planter to bits. #justforfun

16. If you'd like to know where I'll be in the next few days...look for the woman with the pen in her hand, holding a leather bound notebook, tears streaming down her cheeks, listening to Celtic music.

17. What's your profundity for today?

It's Sunday. Another day to love. Happy Sunday.

Out of suffering have emerged the strongest souls; the most massive characters are seared with scars.

Kahlil Gibran

December

Sunday Morning Ramblings: December 2015

1. It's been a weekend. Let's just say that I could have written these ramblings at 2am, for real. 2am. #morningramblings

2. We've all decided that the trinity is Me, Myself and I. And it does appear to be hole-y. And oneness is being self-centered. #freeyourself #therestwillfollow

3. It's really easy to check in with yourself to see what your motives are. Brave people do this all the time. #livebrave

4. I saw the light. Again. #Iwillfacethesetruths

5. If someone is telling you not to question them, or their actions...be bold and do it anyway. Your ego will get harmed in the process. That will be one of the best things that will ever happen to you. #letgomyEGO

6. I sat with WITH some of the most gorgeous, honest folks last night...right here in my living room speaking about what is real. Love lit up the space. #neverregretLOVE #neverregretHONESTY

7. I believe real friendship to be a privilege, crossing divides, healing tragedies, offering hope on levels no mind can comprehend. And belly laughs are in the same category. #lovetheonesyouarewith

8. Liars come in all shapes, sizes, flavors, colors, traditions...hard to tell what is what. Love on the other hand, when it arrives YOU SIMPLY KNOW IT. And when IT LEAVES...the sound is crushing. #beLOVE

9. Adventure is absolutely everything it's supposed to be.

10. I don't say "I want" any longer. Instead, I just wait. #calmliving

11. We are uncovering what's been concealed. #wowzers #glorystory

12. Friends. #takesonetoknowone

13. Relationships. #takesonetohaveone

14. Dogs. #Ijustwantedtotypethat

15. 'Tis the Season of Being...and doing, of course. Cuz double ovens make a girl smile on baking day!

16. 'Tis also the Season of Napping.

It's Sunday. Another day to love. Happy Sunday.

Sunday Morning Ramblings: December 2015

1. Next Sunday it will be the New Year. So this Sunday I'd like to reflect on this past year, which is still the current year. #mindmeld

2. I'm trying to remember this year. Wait. Hold on. It's coming to me. #livingmoreinthemoment #lol

3. Every year, every day...heck, every moment I learn something. I was once told that I have a desire for deep understanding. I won't argue with that. But I will try to understand it. lol Understanding myself more clearly helps me understand others. Parents know this simply by watching their children. Each child being completely different from their siblings. We parent our sons very differently. If the entire Universe and all its contents were the same - besides everything being really dull and boring - the cookie cutter approach to child rearing would be just that - then systems would work efficiently all the time. But nothing, not one single thing in this life is cookie cutter. Not a system. Not a people. Not a person. And my desire to understand these wonderful differences has brought me to this conclusion: Relationship to one another and living in the moment, connected to the source, is by far the happiest and most contented life. #stayconnected

4. I love Love in all its simplicities and complexities.

5. Oh right 2015. Ramblings, remember? I can't think of a single thing to reflect on...oh wait...

6. I was recently at a holiday party with a group of folks I don't know very well. One conversation led to another and then something totally perplexing happened. The box of truth and

experience opened up. Standing in the room with me were an entire group of people, all sharing personal experiences about leaving churches they used to attend. They all felt that something wasn't right with the "churches" and the pastors/staff. Some had attended these churches for many years. Others had belonged to many churches over the years Each of these people had left because of a feeling, gut instinct, their spirit whatever you'd like to call it - because they were referring to IT with many different names - told them something wasn't RIGHT, later to find out the pastors/staff were dealing with questionable doings and goings on with parishoners, or within the organization, or there were doctrinal errors. Now that probably doesn't surprise many. But this is the clincher...at least for me: They are ALL being shunned in their communities. SHOCKED! They also were told that the pastors were preaching lies about them from the platform, calling them "evil" - really?!? Truly nothing new under the sun. But my takeaway here: GET SOME NEW MATERIAL! #everybody

7. I used to read everything spiritual I could get my hands on. Then I had a couple of babies and well...life went to the library for Bob The Builder and Harry Potter...I digress. Truth is truth. Period. In the Bible it states, "Those that seek the truth, find it." Trust me on this one. If you're truly looking to uncover THE TRUTH, you will have to be BRAVE. It is NOT for the faint of heart. It is a crucial uncovering that will ALTER one's life dramatically. Mine happened while I was in a church or because of one. I think wherever the LIE is the GREATEST is when a

spirit canNOT live that way any longer. But not everyone's TRUTH SEEKING happens because of or in a church. No cookie cutter living, remember? The catalyst can be while in a relationship or dealing with the aftermath of bad choices and the list goes on. However the SPIRITUAL JOURNEY is a private matter. It's yours and ONLY yours. #bebrave

8. Speaking of finding one's voice..wait, was I? Well, I am. We all have one, you know? You know you've found yours if you aren't regurgitating someone else's words, but have dug deep into the darkest places of yourself, removed the debris, gotten to the root and begun gently caressing the bits that were shattered and crumbled. I can tell you this from my personal experience. It sucks. It hurts. It's deeply uncomfortable. You may feel like you have to start all over again. Because you will. #beginnings

9. I love people. But now that I TRUST my voice and my soul, I choose whom I share space with. I will only be with those who I can have a true relationship with. Anything else wastes everyone's time. #meaningful #friendships #family

10. My answers are not everyone's answers. Nor are our questions all the same.

11. This past year there have been mended hearts and healed relationships. #oldfriends #grateful #bravepeople

12. If you can BE LOVE, you are a gifted human being.

13. Are these reflections?

14. I have eaten more carbs in the past month than I have throughout this entire year. There. A reflection. #smiles #bloated

15. I am grateful that some of you come here to read these ramblings. It warms my heart and also helps me heal. Thank you.

16. As in 2000 and... Here's to a lovely ending of another twirl around the Sun.

It's Sunday. Another day to love. Happy Sunday.

For small creatures such as we the vastness is bearable only
through love.

Carl Sagan

2016

January

1. Happy New Year, the whole entire year. And if not the whole 365 days...then many of those days but most definitely some grand and wild and lovely moments. #payattentiontothespaceyouarein

2. I've noticed simply looking up or looking down changes my perspective instantaneously. And sometimes makes me a little dizzy. #dontmovetooquickly

3. Carry your head and heart with gentle grace. Your soul will be ever-so grateful. #soulsmatter #itisYOURsoul

4. If God is truly a puppeteer over the entire Universe, I'm not sure I would get along with that form. However, when we go against our true nature it's as if those strings get all tied in knots and we need to cut them loose. Understanding the ebb and flow of the true nature of living creates a deep peace. It's beautiful to be a part of that flow. And gosh, we know when we are going against it; stuck in the eddy without boat or paddle, and no head gear! #becareful

5. If you are telling people what to believe...sorry...YOU ARE WRONG. It's just simple math, really. Your belief + My belief =

Potential Disaster. I used to know a woman who told her controlling husband (now divorced), "The day you walk in my skin is the day you can have a say." Amen! I've learned through a harsh life lesson that holding onto beliefs is a form of a self-prison sentence - keeping yourself out and everyone else, too. #youknowitonsomelevel #beenthere #swallowyourpride #youwilllivethroughit #admissionsFREEyoucompletely

6. I met this really cool lady a couple of weeks ago. She's in her 80's and has her nose pierced. Gosh. Freedom, people. Freedom to live. #letsgetfree #yourTRUELIFEmatters #piercingisNOTthepoint

7. This year it's the album and the book, I think. #creations #ARThasitsOWNvoice #tryingtolisten

8. The only resolution I can EVER truly make is to be me - flawed, silly, loving, caring, introspective, challenged, whimsical. #noOneElseCanDoIt

9. I love the people in my life. #grateful

10. I stopped "being friends" with some folks here on FB. I've read these gals' blogs for a million years but something inside me told me to stop...when the followers start worshiping the person and EVERYTHING they say and do...well, it starts to get creepy. Is this human nature? If so, it's the flawed bit.

#IdontbelievepoliticiansSAVEeither #asmuchasIlovethesegals
#gottago #dontputpeopleonpedestals #please

11. I don't have the answers for you. Sorry. I barely have them for myself. I am, however, learning more and more to pay close attention to the voice within.

12. I used to want to be a model. I'm tall. That's all.

13. When I was in 7th grade I entered a "talent" contest. I didn't have any talent. I responded to an advertisement in the newspaper. The only line I thought was important stated that the contestants would be asked how to make the world a better place. At 13yo, I must have thought I had the answer. So, I filled out the application. My outfit of choice: a lemon yellow one piece pant suit with kelly green ric rac trim, tan wedge sandals on my feet. Sitting with girls my age and younger, their hair all done up, makeup on their faces, I began to sweat. My hair style was circa 1976 Keith Partridge. My makeup? Wide Grape Bonne Bell lip gloss. Grandma and Mom sat in the back of the room. The "talent" people lined us all up on stage. We were asked to walk around in front of them. Then a panel asked us questions. I didn't win or even get chosen. The woman in charge publicly announced why. She did that to all the girls who didn't get picked. She used the words awkward and non-athletic. She praised the girls she chose and announced why, "beautiful posture" "lovely skin." She told me (what was left of me) that I had some very serious responses to the questions. She was

impressed with that. "Don't enter any more pageants. They're not for you. Go out and change the world." The contest? The Miss Teen New York State Beauty something or other. #eyeroll #mortified #livedtotellaboutit40yearslater

14. Now go do what you can for this scared world. Love it. Care for it. Its contents are the most precious. #love

It's Sunday. Another day to love. Happy Sunday

Sunday Morning Ramblings: January 2016

(This song is for two of our friends and their perfectly sweet family. We can't be there to sit and hold your hands and melt into your pain with you. However, we are rising for you. We love you. *Here I shared the song, Rise Up by Andra Day)

1. When the heart needs mending, the mind takes over completely. But we cannot live with simply the brain doing all the work, all the decisions, all the caring. We need the heart. Even science supports this. The broken heart may still beat. Yet, the two need each other to live...whole; mind and heart. The mind is actually weakened without the heart. It becomes entangled in a matrix with the false idea that all decisions and authority can be derived from its current state. But only until the heart begins to mend can the brain relax and function properly.

An awakening occurs. It appears to be a miracle. Because it is. #truehealing

2. I believe in love. Forever.

3. When we TRULY WAKE UP in our lives, the mess we have made will seem unbearable and daunting. It is. But going back to sleep simply cannot be an option. #itwillbeOK #onemomentatatime

4. I love my friends. Forever. #Iwillclimbtheirmountainswiththem

5. When we are broken, and we realize our brokenness, this is truly the only place we can heal and become whole. Otherwise, we are just dragging around pieces of ourselves in a fine looking wagon, pretending. Passersby, staring, mouths agape. Family/friends, doing all they can to make sure those broken bits don't spill out. And the only people to be engaged with us, giving us a false sense of identity will be pulling their own wagons alongside ours. #bewhole

6. I've cried a lot in the last few days. But in the midst of my tears I have seen love. I believe in it. It is the only thing that means anything. Ever. #holdontothat

7. Cruel people have hurt me. Cruel people have hurt you. Interesting though, loving people have done the same. #findthelovers #teachyourselftoforgive #thereisabiggerpicture

8. I'm having many of my girlfriends over this coming weekend. They are a gorgeous array of the finest human beings I know. I am privileged to share the planet with them. #SouperSaturday

9. I started working out again. As I type this, my elbows are propped up with pillows. #inbed #itsMorning #rambling

10. Ok. So there's this thing about bangs. I mean what is the deal? It took me about 6 months to grow mine out. And now I want bangs again. I had to grab the definition. Here 'tis:
Bangs. noun
(bangs) a fringe of hair cut straight across the forehead: she brushed back her wispy bangs. [ORIGIN: from a use of the adverb bang to mean [abruptly.]]
Ok, that must be it. Abruptly. Something is going on and I need to do something ABRUPTLY. Hmm. Not content having the longer hair swaying around my face...hmmm. Psycho-analytical...just a bit...right now. Bear with me. So what did I do? Yesterday I went to the hair shop. (they have hair shops here) I bought some fringe. I did. Crazy. I'm wild like that. My 15yo was with me. Running errands. I said, "I just want to pop in here. Do you think it's weird if I buy bangs?" 'No, Mom, if that's what you want to do." (love him) So I did. And then I nearly bled trying to affix these things onto my head. But boy did they

look cute. Conclusion: I will not be wearing false bangs any time. However, "wispy" I really relate to. #sorryguysthisISaGIRLTHING

11. When something valuable is broken we must do everything we can to mend it.

12. We have so much power within us...to do all sorts of good things. #believeIT

13. My husband just cleaned the kitchen and is now cooking in the kitchen as I type this with my elbows propped up on pillows. Marriage. It can do a body good. #wink

14. Emotions have a way of ruling the world. Emotions also have a way of ruining the world. What is ruling or ruining your world right now? #deepbreaths #growingupishardtodo #period

15. Our very large puppy has no idea that he isn't a cuddle bunny...no idea at all...jumps right into our laps, hugs us, then throws his head back against our chests and looks lovingly up into our faces. I believe LOVE is ruling his world.

It's Sunday. Another day to love. Happy Sunday.

Sunday Morning Ramblings: January 2016

1. Waking up. It's hard to do. Sometimes in the morning.
Sometimes in the night. Sometimes without warning.
Sometimes in the fight. Sometimes without hope. Sometimes
without light. Cover up our head. Pull that blanket up real
close. Left feeling a bit lonely. Or a lot more lost. We can stay
asleep forever. In the bed we've made, we lie. Or begin to crawl
out from this place we've been tied. Draw the drapes. Pick up
some clothes. Grab our shoes. Warm our toes. Notice the pale
sky above. Our heart still beating, Love. Take notice of this
moment. There is no other task. If the pressure gets too great, it
won't last. Deep breaths are plenty. In this place we dwell.
Think good thoughts...begin today...and all will eventually be
well. #lovetoyouduringthesewintermonths

2. And then there's always copious amounts of coffee and dark
chocolate, a nice deep stretch and a really long walk outside...
#notmakinglightofdepression #lovetoyouandmealways

3. I love my neighbors. They are good.

4. I ate two breakfasts this morning. Just for fun.

5. I'm rearranging my life. Again. #lettinggo #cleaningclosets
#movingfurniture

6. Begin. #itisachoice

7. Went to a play last night. Every play I have EVER gone to I
have always left with a feeling that I want to be an actress.

146

"That's it! I'm going to be on the stage!" Last night I compared writing to performing, while sitting there right in my seat. Writing pulled me closer, gave me a hug, a sweet smile. I was glad to be home. #somethingstakeaLONGtimetorealize

8. It's lonely at the top. I've heard. I've never been there. However, I have been lonely. But not at the top. At the bottom, actually. Conclusion: It's lonely at the top and at the bottom. The middle has got it going on! Let's stay there. Together.

9. I'm an onion. Metaphorically speaking…

10. Kissing is fun. Hugging is great, too. But there's something about a cup of hot chocolate that…well…tops everything for me. #midliferealizations #lol

11. It occurred to me last night while sitting next to my very good and wonderful friend that we are living our lives together because our children are in the same age range. I wanted to cry. I also wanted to thank all the gods in the entire Universe that have ever been acknowledged for such a gift. She's a gift. Her family is a gift. I have the best gift of everything in all of them. #tears

12. And here is the thing… I am myself with them and they love and appreciate who I am…in my weakness, in my strength, in my errors, in my challenges…they have NEVER, not ONCE, asked me to change or be "better" or different. They are a gift. #thebestkindoffall

13. Find your gifts. They are precious. #people

14. I still hold out hope that two particular friends from the past will call me. I have an inkling they want to.

15. It's cloudy, and heavy, and wet outside today. I've got a ton of inside stuff to do. How 'bout you?

It's Sunday. Another day to love. Happy Sunday

Sunday Morning Ramblings: January 2016

1. Yoga begins tomorrow. Whole new month. All of February. I'll be posting poses. #agoodstretch

2. I'm growing up into being...a child. #fun #laughter #sweetlove

3. In the moment, if we can stay there long enough, we may just find all we need. #peace #joy

4. I'm finding that a good protein bar can change the grocery store shopping experience. #eat

5. I only LIKE/LOVE to shop for home & garden stuff. Ever. #notfood #notclothes

6. Today I'll be in the studio - organizing...and hopefully creating. #fabricsculptures

7. Clarity and trust walk hand in hand, side by side...and are good, good friends. #beleeryoftheshadowmakers

8. Watch what people do...to others. Then, decide.

9. My animal symbol in Native American culture is an...owl. Who knew? #LOVEthem #alwaysHave #tidbit

10. Life changes slowly and then BAM the shift is so great we fear we'll collide with the wind. Breathe and reset your sails. You will begin to steer again. #time

11. I've been carrying a family in my heart since losing a friend. I find that love is always the answer, no matter what.

12. I've got a pile of books on my bedside table. I'm giddy every night! #library #friendswhoareauthors

13. I worked on my book this month. #aBOOK #PEOPLEaBOOK

14. I love.

It's Sunday. Another to love. Happy Sunday

Sunday Morning Ramblings: January 2016

1. If you have love in ANY area of your life, you are rich. #takenotice

2. Love your past self...don't be too harsh...we do the best we can within each given moment. #care

3. Perfection comes in the moment between two spirits, open with wonder, to receive what the other has to give. #givers

4. Leon Redbone was on vinyl last night. #SouperSaturday

5. I fell in love again last night. #gorgeouswomen

6. Even though some of my true friends are not in my life right now...what we shared was real. I honor that time and space. And love them still. #cult

7. Last night buckets of love were shared between lovely human beings with the most gorgeous spirits. Buckets pouring out, being passed around the room in the form of genuine care and joy and honesty. #loveLove

8. The only boy at the party was Sergeant, our Dutch Shepherd puppy. He made a point of making himself available to all the ladies. #HeisaLOVER

9. ...and girlfriends!!! the food!!!! was amazing!!!!!

10. I'm not cleaning my kitchen until Monday. #sothere

11. I was stressing about cleaning the house beforehand and realized it was residual stuff from *my past life* of the cute/kind version of Mommy Dearest. I put the cleaning supplies down and cut some fresh flowers and placed them in vases and turned on some music and rocked that junk off of me. It was perfect just the way it was. No one walked in and asked if I'd cleaned the toilet. I was shocked. Kidding.

12. When you've moved past the garbage, humor is a wonderful release. #I #love #to #laugh

13. Rocks.

14. Ramblings.

15. Rumblings. #ohisitlunchtime

It's Sunday. Another day to love. Happy Sunday.

Sometimes people don't want to hear the truth because they don't want their illusions destroyed.

Friedrich Nietzsche

February

Sunday Morning Ramblings: February 2016

1. When I decided to be a mother, just a few years ago or maybe
it was a few months ago..oh wait, it may have been
yesterday...everything changed. I know, I'm here to confuse
you. Officially, biologically I became a mother the nano-second
I learned I was pregnant. However BEING a mother is a whole
different reality. You see there is this pressure to be the BEST
mother or the IT mother or the MOTHER OF ALL AND
EVERYTHING BEST DESIGNER MOTHER or the MOTHER
WHO DOES IT ALL MOTHER. Or the pressure to STAY
HOME MOTHER (but that's a whole other MOTHER, if you
know me for the last two years...Oy, churches wreak havoc in
the lives of kind and peaceful people...I digress). BEING a
mother, Mom, Momma or Mommy, Mum has more to do with
our daily, minute to minute decision as a Mother than it does
with who's screaming our new name from the other room.
BEING a mother. I decided to do that. And my whole life
changed. And the lives of my children changed. The lives of
my dogs changed too. Funny that. So, here I am getting all
philosophical...nope. Not even a little. Funny that. The new
reality takes place in the moment, with the need, in BEING
present. Not buying presents, of any sort. Of course we all
KNOW this already. Geesh. But BEING is not easy. It means

there is a PAUSE button (we've all got one - somewhere). I had to dig for mine. Recently a vent from my gorgeous sister brought LIGHT to some memories I had detached myself from. These were GOOD memories. (we detach ourselves from good memories - let's stop doing that) The people who helped develop the BEST in me were the BEINGS. They were PRESENT. I can count them on one hand. Actually, I can count them on two fingers. That's it. Two. Two PRESENT BEINGS doing mundane tasks. Chop Wood, Carry Water. ENLIGHTENMENT. That's it. Of course all these answers are TRULY SIMPLE. We, as non-BEINGS, make them difficult. BECAUSE WE GET IN THE WAY OR WE KICK AND SCREAM TO GET OUR WAY OR WE KICK LOVELY PEOPLE OUT OF OUR WAY thinking they are the troublemakers..."If only....blah, blah, blah...then I'd BE!" NOPE. We will BE only when we are BEING. PRESENT, that is. And there is no other way. No book, no group, no counselor...it's YOU. It's ME. BEING. HERE. RIGHT NOW. MOTHER.

2. Don't let mean people decide your fate. Find the kind ones. Hang with them. You'll save your life. #andkeepliving

3. I'm currently penning two books. One a fiction. The other a reality. As I write, the thought of the outfit I'm wearing at my first book signing keeps displaying itself in my head. #huh? #IamALLaboutTHEbookSIGNING #huh?

4. There's a line in a song that I wrote (or it wrote itself - I can't figure out inspiration) - "Enlighten my load." That's it, really. #lightenUP #me

5. Pain is horrible. Any kind. I remember the doula firmly telling me, as my body contracted during childbirth..."Push through the pain." New life happened after that. #gettingphilosophicalNOW

6. I'm not one to follow systems. Systems fail. #evenBELIEFsystems

7. We've been studying the history of Jesus and where and why the Bible was formed. Do you know there is no REAL, as in FACTUAL history of Jesus? #rockedmyworld #morereasontotrusttheSPIRITwithin #truefaith

8. I felt lonely at first. Then, I didn't. #changeishard #backtofaith

9. There are great truths in the Bible. There is also great confusion in the Bible. #being #present #moment #truthwithin

10. Ramblings.

11. If we are holding on too tightly to anything, chances are something will happen to assist in loosening our grip. Then, we may have the privilege of experiencing "letting go" - or not. It is still a choice. #choosetoletgo

12. Seeking the truth is NOT for the faint of heart. #brave #tears

13. Today I need to go stare at the trees, up into them, where the sky meets and greets and the sun dangles hope between each branch and simply BE.

14. And smile.

It's Sunday. Another day to love. Happy Sunday.

Sunday Morning Ramblings: February 2016

1. Persnickety is the sort of word that makes me think of nuts and caramel and chocolate, my tongue on a constant excavation in my mouth searching for tiny bits and the reward being the release of sweet and bitter. #yepitistrue

2. I made banana bread and banana muffins last night using almond flour, coconut oil and a tad of honey. #scrumptious #protein

3. Moving on will only happen after we move through. If you stomp your feet and mess up your hair and shout, "I'm so done with that!" Guess what? You aren't. It's ok. You're getting close. #movingthroughthepainandsorrow

4. It's good to be you. #pleasedonotstop

5. My 15yo listens to music on his ipad...a lot. Yesterday, it was Michael Jackson's Man in the Mirror. "Yeah, yeah, yeah, yeah, nananaanananana...ahuh...nananaaanananana...make that change."

6. Fear has its proper place in my life now. It no longer has the power to stop me. I'm a pretty cautious person anyway; this gift comes from being sensitive and a mother caring for her children. #makenoapologiesforwhoyouare

7. When I used to go to a place called *a church* it was drilled into our heads that the world was evil and bad and awful and vile and sickening and...well, let's just say the whole place of "worship" was on fire burning with such awful, venomous

156

judgment. Constantly being troubled by this nearly broke me. I never believed it. I couldn't. It hurt my spirit. And since I've not been screamed at now for a few years I've realized that if there is beauty and love inside of you, that's what you find...all around. Thank God. #wemirrorwhatweare #lessons

8. Nowhere I go now does anyone scream at me. For this sensitive being, there is such relief. It makes me cry. Then I smile. #thanktheUniverse

9. As I walked down the street, in an artsy part of town after meeting a friend for lunch the other day, a man stood tucked in between two buildings. Just as I passed he popped out and asked if I had 50 cents. (I never carry cash with me) I paused, turned and looked him right in the eye. "No I don't. I never have cash on me." We stared at each other, completely connected for a few seconds. He nodded his head like a proper gentleman, thanked me, then wished me a good day. #theworld

10. I am a writer. I don't write for others' eyes or hearts or opinions or critiques. I write for my own. I need to write for my own. #heal #change #awareness #living #heart

11. However, if you are taking the time to read this, thank you.

12. A little peace goes a long way. A lot of peace makes a way.

13. I'm still healing. How about you?

14. I love people.

It's Sunday. Another day to love. Happy Sunday.

In a gentle way you can shake the world.

Gandhi

march

Sunday Morning Ramblings: March 2016

1. TRUTH and LIES

2. As I sit and type these ramblings on a Sunday morning there is *a preacher* standing up on a platform spewing LIES about my family and a bunch of my friends. They're lies. All of them. I write this because LIES are everywhere these days, more so than the average day. And while I find all of this incredulous, I also find it alarming, and sometimes, even funny.

3. However, there remains a compass within each of us that steers us to placid waters or at least a clarity of mind and heart where we can rest with our thoughts, in our decisions. My resting place is different than yours. Or maybe it's the same. Your journey takes you to places and paths emotionally, spiritually, politically that mine may never cross. And the same can be said for every one of us. It is in this difference that we are the same. Our similarity is what makes us human, even if - gasp - we REALLY disagree with each other.

4. I've read alarming LIES about people lately in the political arena. It's terrible and sad. TRUTH rarely sells. It's a shame because I think the TRUTH is crazy and wonderful and makes the best flippin' stories without embellishment. So I'll write some

books and more poetry. Gotta get the TRUTH out there somehow, right? Do what YOU can, too!

5. I digress. I bring this up because a clear decision I made one day based on the TRUTH within me (which, by the way, is one of the best decisions I have ever made...and don't get me started on the lives of our two young sons) has become fodder for LIES of an entire congregation and its leaders. My TRUTH does not make my decision any less than their decision to stay in such a place. Maybe the folks who stay don't see or sense what I sensed. Perhaps the risk of losing their community is too great. Others may stay because they married into *the family*. If they leave they lose their daughter or son or grandchildren. And the leaders stay because they garner attention, money and power. Some cannot give that up no matter the personal trial they find themselves in.

6. All of this is said to express something deeper: If we, as people, do not TRUST THE TRUTH that dwells within us, what are we here for? Don't be swayed by external voices that interfere with your inside truth. If we give up our personal power to *feed* the group's opinion or an individual's opinion, who carries the burden? Ultimately we do. Individually. Collectively. If we do not honor our personal decisions and give them the space and attention they deserve then we actually harm those around us - not to mention ourselves.

7. It's the authentic life, flawed as it may be, that makes way for creation, freedom, liberties, care and possibilities. No matter who lies about us, who fabricates story after story, who re-creates an altered reality to suit their agenda we remain capable and

strong knowing that our decisions are made from a place of PERSONAL TRUTH. And no one can ever take that from you. That personal truth weaves a story so beautiful, unique and rich.

8. Never allow your TRUTH to lie dormant so long that your voice is a mere distant echo. Speak your truth, whatever that may be, in whatever moment it presents itself. All the TRUTH SEEKERS are waiting with bated breath. They WILL hear you. And they WILL thank you.

It's Sunday Another day to love Happy Sunday

Sunday Morning Ramblings: March 2016

1. Do you know anyone who might have a Messiah complex? Many people do...from all walks of life - those who claim they are full of love for humanity and those who are full of hate from infancy. It's based on grand delusions. In people where it is allowed to fester, the person is usually diagnosed as schizophrenic. People in power who have this complex- ooph....look out!

2. If a tree limb falls on your house and damages your roof do you:
a. blame the tree
b. blame the earth
c. blame humanity
d. cut down the DYING tree

Why?

3. Today in many parts of the world people believe that a man rose from the dead. When anyone wakes up to their failings, their self-lies, their darkness and walks into the light - he or she has risen. Self-examination is death and can free us from our pride and arrogance which IS the grand delusion. The process is extremely painful and realigns us in a way where we face ourselves and decide...do I continue serving my arrogance or do I let it go and have peace from here on out?

4. Taking care of the world. How could I or anyone else possibly know how to do this? If you think YOU know, re-read #1. As a parent of two completely different sons I have learned that each one needs me in a different form. While still in the role of mother I speak to each of my sons with separate approaches. Each of them has a different learning style. One throws all his school books all over the living room floor, papers everywhere. Then proceeds to neatly and succinctly complete every subject, then placing them into his backpack or on the shelf. The other sits calmly at his desk focused. He doesn't usually put his books away. He's visual, likes to see them in his room. Also, the way they get their needs met at times is in contrast to the other. Except for eating. They both do that pretty much the same. Any parent recognizes the constant adjusting that goes on for each child. However, in order for the home to function as a whole there has to be some basic, BASIC, rules keeping balance and harmony. If one side

of the scale falls we immediately adjust to regain balance...otherwise, the possibility for brokenness soars and the chances of harmony are lost. So then, what about the world?

5. Both my sons are given a chance at "life, liberty and the pursuit of happiness." Once they have finished college/skill training and move out of the house, they are free to "pursue happiness" - happiness as defined by their spirit, soul, and mind NOT by anyone else. I pray.

6. Pursue. Which definition should be the most suitable for people, the world, our neighbors, friends, officials in government, third world villagers, business men and women, Unicorn believers?

Definition 1? "follow someone or something with the plan of attack, persistently afflict someone"

OR

Definition 2? "continue or proceed along (a path or route), engage in (an activity or course of action) continue to investigate, explore, or discuss."

7. If someone attacked you or your family in any way, what would you do? Christians are told to "offer the other cheek" - does anyone really think this is going to work?

8. Are you free, right now, this minute? What is freedom to you?

9. What we put into our minds and bodies has a great effect on us. I spent the last several months reading and learning about the political arena. While some people may thrive in this information it damaged me. I was broken. I learned more about power and greed than I care to. I had to pick the pieces of myself up and heal. Not all was lost. I realized more about myself, my choices, my decisions in life. I learned that I have the ability to be objective. I learned that the way I love people, as poetic as I am, is based in reality and concrete ways more so than fantasy or high mindedness. I've sifted through all sides, paid attention, listened without judgment. It wasn't easy at first but became easier as I became more defined. I also realized...I don't have all the answers.

10. Leaving *religion* has been such an awakening. The dawning may burn one's eyes at first. However, having true sight is actually quite beautiful. Loving and accepting people and all their beliefs is so much more freeing than before.

11. I won't be giving up poetry... anytime soon.

12. I live a really simple life. Feeding my sons, throwing some paint on a canvas every now and again, teaching, training, writing, singing, seeing friends and family, an occasional date with my guy and letting the dogs out a million times a day.

And a good long walk in the park a few times a week. That's really about it.

13. I'm only driven to love and to write. Everything else I do is based on the needs of others or myself.

14. These are ramblings. If my words offend please know it is never my heart's intention, as I write to understand myself and others.

15. I really do love...more than anything else.

It's Sunday. Another day to love. Happy Sunday.

We must accept finite disappointment but never lose infinite hope.

Martin Luther King, Jr.

April

Sunday Morning Ramblings: April 2016

1. Well, I'm finally convinced. Everything...takes time.

2. Our journeys are unique and wonderful. When our paths cross with some people it might be more like a head-on collision or a fork in the eye. This is clearly when it's time to change directions; after you pull the fork out, of course. You'll need your vision for the rest of the journey. #metaphormomma

3. Making a choice means freedom is saddled up close with a sweet grin, while the pull cord dangles in the wind. #youAREgonnaFLY

4. I've been thinking about forgiveness, a lot. Forget is usually coupled with that word. Forgive. Forget. So far my conclusion is forgetting is nearly impossible. And forgiving a close second. Moving forward seems to be the only way, making sure there are millions of miles between you and that hurt. What about forgiving ourselves? I've given that some thought, too (ha!). This I believe is possible by pouring into our life as much love and kindness and creativity as a life can hold. And bit by bit we begin to like ourselves again and feel lighter. #letgo

5. Hang with good people, the people who care for you in that particular way that keeps you YOU.

6. I met a posse of new friends the other night. No kidding. It was a posse. These woman had been there, done it - more than once and lived to tell about it. They are a posse of perfected power! #whoababy #newfriends #excited

7. What do you need today? Sometimes a simple whisper out into the atmosphere can make a difference. #goaheadASK

8. Today. Right now. It's a gift.

9. These are ramblings...

10. I've been reading Goddesses Never Age. It's directing me somewhere. I can feel it.

11. The sun is proving itself right now. However, the temperature got the date wrong. Stay cozy!

It's Sunday. Another day to love. Happy Sunday.

Sunday Morning Ramblings: April 2016

1. FreeToFindPearls performed yesterday. That's my band. I have a band? I have a band.

2. Music is another part of the expression of my life through art. #sograteful #writer

3. I love the musicians in my band. I have a band?

4. I had my outfit picked out weeks ago for this gig. That's how I roll. It's all about the outfit. I've done this for forever. If I get the outfit set in my mind then I can focus on the other preparations -

like say, practicing the songs. The clothes are part of the art expression, too, for me. #weareALLart #expressyourSELF #ILOVEgettingdressedUP

5. My guy took me out to a fancy dinner last night after our gig. Just the two of us. #heartsinging

6. Oh. And. Everything takes time. #justalittleweeklyreminder

7. Waiting is hard. It's sometimes lonely. But never give up on where your beautiful dreams take you in your mind. There is a reason you are dreaming those dreams. The world NEEDs those dreams to materialize. We need you...all of you...not just a portion because the rest may be too pie-in-the-sky so that bit doesn't have to show up. No way! Keep dreaming ALL of those dreams...keep them alive. Choose the outfit way ahead of time.

8. EC has offered to build me a she-shed/artist studio. I cried. Then I squealed. #manofmydreams

9. My sons performed yesterday with their band. They have a band? Wait. I have sons?

10. I am in awe of my sons for expressing who they are, right now, in this moment. #beauties #realpeople

11. Kind people have a way of being kind. Always. If the group they're hanging with has ulterior motives, then the kind people must move on. It's ok to move on. Really. #facingthetruth

12. There's this little area just outside my bedroom window, that if I'm at the right angle looking out it reminds me of an English garden. #joy

13. People don't get to decide anything about your life. Your life is yours. #BeBOLD

14. These are ramblings.

15. If you don't want to talk to someone, you don't have to. Take a deep breath and walk on by...

It's Sunday. Another day to love. Happy Sunday.

The soul has been given its own ears to hear the things the mind does not understand.

rumi

may

Sunday Morning Ramblings: May 2016

1. There's this belief that we all need to be "better"...at just about everything from how we do our hair, to how we decorate our home, organize a drawer, dress, breathe, move, speak...how about this idea? You are grand just the way you are.

2. "Do what you have to until you can do what you want to." This has to be my mantra. I've got young sons. I refuse to jump on the pressure train speeding down the highway to stress any longer. I was put here for a reason or several reasons. I must allow the universe, my universe, to unfold in its allotted time. And not, I repeat, NOT, get in its way.

3. Trust that who you are, what you're doing right now is absolutely everything that is needed. And breathe.

4. Letting go is pretty amazing.

5. Be blessed by what is in front of you. #love

6. Getting back in touch with my deep spirituality is truly who I am. #writing #prayer #visions #dreams

7. If I could move out of this area I would in a heartbeat. I don't enjoy living here anymore. Too much pain. Not enough joy. But alas, the Universe says to wait. So I wait. #getawayanyone?

8. Working on putting together two books at the same time is actually quite fun.

9. Planning on a Goddess Garden Party possibly in June. Anyone interested?

10. My She-Shed has turned into a possible addition on the house. #ohmy #ideas #quotes #giddy #vision

11. Don't let them worry you. They are nothing. If you've got LOVE and RELATIONSHIP you've got everything.

12. Spiritual writing is one of my gifts.

13. Gifts are to be shared.

14. Be who you are today. We need you.

It's Sunday. Another day to love. Happy Sunday

Sunday Morning Ramblings: May 2016

1. I'm reflecting today. #love

2. If the start of something new was meant to be, is it truly a new beginning or simply a part of the gorgeous continuum of life? #love

3. I love love. #love

4. Can you tell we went to a wedding yesterday? #giddy

5. And then there's this: We ramble through life, tripping and bumping into stuff/people/lessons and we still get another crack

at it. Every day. Another crack. Another chance to engage or understand or trip, pick ourselves up, brush the junk off and carry on. This is the clincher, though. It is through the creative choices that we make every moment whether or not we participate in #2. Because we certainly can choose to remain stuck. And in "stuck" we may lose our creative self. But surely, at any given time (time is given), we can creatively choose something/anything to move us forward...and find a new beginning on the continuum in this thing called life. #beginagain

6. I met a young woman many years ago and I knew we would always love each other. She got married yesterday. *tears #souls

7. The table I sat at yesterday was a table of friends whose story is intermingled with a depth of truth and knowledge that far outreaches any other. I used to dream of such a relationship to others. My dreams are coming true. #holdontothosedreams #theydonothappenbythemselves #letpeoplein #staypresent

8. Oh and did I mention that EC and I "cut up some rug" yesterday? Yes, we did! #danced #wearechanged #greatjoy

9. Yesterday I ironed clothes. I haven't done that in 3 years. #justsaying #freedomhaswrinkles

10. If someone is constantly telling you that you're free and you feel like you're in shackles, guess what? You're in shackles. Slave owners told the people who lived on their plantations they were free, too. #whenyouareAFRAIDyouareNOTfree

11. But let's dwell on LOVE instead. Because, baby, there ain't nothing else like it! #love #YAYLOVE

12. Go get yourself some love today. Or better yet. Go give some!!!

It's Sunday. Another day to love. Happy Sunday.

Sunday Morning Ramblings: May 2016

1. Ramblings was postponed because this teeny bug crawled into our family and knocked us out - or at least tried to - no sleep, sipping broth and lots of boxes of tissue. #achoo

2. Speaking the truth...let's talk about that...when I embarked on this writing journey here publicly on FB my voice shook. It shook for many reasons. One of them had to do with speaking the truth.

3. Does truth set us free? I'm not sure.

4. What I think really happens if we are stuck, say in shackles or chains, which God forbid, none of you are, remember that, but mental shackles and chains - and we hear or sense the truth, it doesn't make us free.

5. At the worst it makes us shake. At best and with possibility the truth opens a door - perhaps a door to a cell, a prison.

6. And some of us wait.

7. Some of us don't walk through because the prison is all we've known.

8. Some of us peek around the corner from time to time.

9. And some of us slide back in and grab our grey wool blanket and lay our heads down on the ticking fabric covered pillows and cot and figuratively suck our thumb.

10. When I learned the truth about *the religion* I had devoted myself to for a 3rd of my life I began to shake. My voice didn't shake because I didn't have a voice. Yet. My inner being shook. It trembled. All the stages of emotions of grief ran their course - a few times over.

11. We may get run over, too.

12. But we may just find our lives and live.

It's Sunday. Another day to love. Happy Sunday.

Ever since happiness heard your name, it has been running
through the streets trying to find you.

Hafiz

June

Sunday Morning Ramblings: June 2016

1. It's morning...again...we get another whole entire day to
do,
be,
grow,
learn
and
love.

2. Playing badminton with my 12yo yesterday? Such fun!

3. Two Messianic Jewish folks were walking down the street last night and approached our oldest. After a few minutes of chatter they asked, "Have you accepted JC as your Lord and Savior?" Being respectful and clear, he answered them. "I know who I am." #lovetruth They talked a bit more about music and he was on his way home.

4. The Jehovah's don't stop by our house anymore, I remarked to my husband. #hemayhavespokenLOVEtothem #smile

5. We live in a little multi-faith, multi-lifestyle, multi-cultural hub here in our neighborhood. I personally love it. People are gorgeous - whatever they believe. I love them all.

6. Periodically, I find myself looking through the mini-clothing rack set up in the local pharmacy or grocer. Yesterday I bought a dress. I bought a grocery store dress. I love it!!! Of course when I put it on to show EC he thought it was nightgown. LOL #fashion

7. The guy, our guy, our contractor extraordinaire guy came over the other day....weeeeeeeeeeee! #addition #quote #hesuggestedaFrenchDoor #bestillmyheart

8. Waiting is hard to do. Just do it. And keep hoping. I realize this goes against all the 7 Habits of Highly Successful people mantras. I don't care. Wait. Simply wait. The Universe/God has a rhythm. It's beautiful and melodic and we are one of its symphonic notes. Don't screw up the concert with your noise. Get into the flow. Now if you've been out of the flow, getting in is difficult. Agreed. But never impossible. #bangingonthedrumsalldaywillnotwork

9. I miss my paternal grandmother. She was strong and loved to laugh. Her influence in my life, saved it. With Mars in retrograde, we'll all be feeling old feels. I'm gonna bless them all...even the difficult and strained ones. But especially the lovely ones.

10. The Universe is sending us signs and wonders every flippin' second. Let's not miss a thing. But definitely ask, if you haven't noticed any. You'll get your answer.

11. I adore my sweet little family. Two boys. My best friend. And our two dogs. #Igotmyselfafamily

12. Lessons aren't always easy to learn. I believe they are called Hard Lessons. But not all lessons are deemed to be difficult; especially if we can learn them the first time, eh? #ohboy #Iamaslowlearner #stayOpentoLearning

13. I find it interesting that I'm being led to work on my core. #pilates #taichi #strengthtraining #nocoincidence #Ijustnoticedthis #metaphor

14. Any suggestions for some good, capable flip flops?

15. Goddess Garden Party is in the works. #friends #IwillbeinvitingEVERYONE

It's Sunday. Another day to love. Happy Sunday.

Some of us think hanging on makes us strong but sometimes it is letting go.

Hermann Hesse

July

Sunday Morning Ramblings: July 2016

1. I found out this weekend that we can "go back" - in time, in heart with the people we LOVED.

2. In that place, that going back, we see that what we had was more precious than we realized.

3. The gift of that awareness shines new light, new hope, new beginnings as we gather up those experiences and create more life, more hope and more beginnings.

4. Laughter diminishes nothing.

5. In fact, the cells of the soul are regenerated.

It's Sunday. Another day to love. Happy Sunday

Sunday Morning Ramblings: July 2016

1. Liz Gilbert. I've written to her several times. I delete the words, every time. I suppose I have no words. My heart, however, is beating compassion for her and this enormous shift. This is the time for a shift. #canyoufeelit #letgo #timetomoveon

2. Change is bloody hard. Period.

3. T o all our lovely friends/family who are or have suffered a separation or divorce I can only imagine that twisted knot in the core of your being will eventually, with time and love, begin to loosen; the scar left behind becoming a strength in your being, right there in the center, where YOU begin. #loveheals

4. And then Love walks into a room...

5. Let Love in. Please.

6. Even if you find that Love, is you.

7. Gardening is not in my DNA. I'd much rather RUN through a field of wild flowers. #onmykneesyesteday #pullingweeds

8. These are ramblings...

9. There is a relational shift happening. Those who are sensitive to it will feel it. Let it be. And what needs to go...let that go. It'll be alright.

10. I have been gifted with many things. You have, too.

11. Summer has begun at our house. The volleyball net is a fixture in the yard. The pool is open. The bikes are at the ready. The kayaks will be hosed off. And the spray paint cans are lined up!! #ohthankalltheheavens #schoolisout

12. Tomorrow we celebrate freedom. I celebrate it everyday. #3years

13. Be kind to yourself.

14. Be kind to yourself.

15. Be kind to yourself.

It's Sunday. Another day to love. Happy Sunday

The true hero is one who conquers his own anger and hatred.

Dalai Lama

August

Sunday Morning Ramblings: August 2016

1. Rambling is good.

2. I decided to be radical, more radical than usual with LOVE. It is for the giving, right? If it stays knotted up inside of us...like say...forever...is it truly love at all?

3. So. The other day, before my feet landed on the floor, I told the Universe that I would start LOVING Hilary Clinton and Donald Trump. Radical.

4. Nothing major happened, at first.

5. Then, something shifted. I wasn't angry anymore. Poof. Gone.

6. Then something else happened. I started seeing them as people; simply a woman and a man.

7. Love is pretty darn amazing. When we choose love we become a protector of that love. We stand in front of it. We're braver people because of it. We all fundamentally understand that pointing fingers at someone means there are 3 of our own pointing back at us. Perhaps we should deal with those first. Love thyself, eh?

8. My first pointed finger was about making someone accountable for hurting humanity. Digging deep wasn't needed

185

for this one. I've been hurt, deeply. If you stop by here regularly, you know what happened to us. There are correlations and similarities, albeit in a microcosm, of what raging egos and greed look like. I know someone on the dole who would sell her children to win the lottery. These are weaknesses. Not strengths. Because I want good to win over evil and so far I don't see enough evidence, I thought if I stood on my soapbox pointing out the wrongs, good would prevail. It doesn't. At least not in one collective rush. But I am willing to be the good I am desperate to see in this world. I fail. A lot. But am always willing.

9. The second pointed finger had to do with the many friends who name call and post uninformed memes based on what the media says about a person. How wearisome. Being the subject of lies and mockery myself really got me on this one. I'd go and fact check all this nonsense only to discover a perspective and truth so far from their point that I began considering whether or not these were the folks I desired in "my tribe." I told myself, "be careful" - these folks are angry, hurt and these political figures are easy targets. The one caveat is that we can't process our pain by spewing pain at an untouchable target. I tried. It doesn't work. Learning that my family and I are lied about and name called and shunned and whateverthefreakelse, I've found there is nothing anyone can do...other than wait for karma to have its day. But clearing my house of the rage has got to be #1 in life...otherwise there is NO LIFE.

10. The third finger wasn't obvious...it's the pinky...the small guy. Ah. There you have it. I'm a small guy. I'm the light voice in the room. What do people on the tallest platform in the world choose to say? They are heard by everyone. Much of what is said is distorted, if you listen to the Media God. But listen to your own voice. Your voice is important, as is mine. Perhaps our platforms are smaller. But we have them, just the same. What do you choose to say? And most importantly, what do you do to make this world, this speck of a planet better? Don't leave everything in the hands of others. Are you simply a paper tiger roaring or do you take some self-appointed action and love the ones you're with? It's science. LOVE and HATE cannot occupy the same space.

11. And then I thought, what if on my worst day, you ALL got a glimpse into who I am? Oh boy, would there be memes!

12. I'm going to give Hilary Clinton the benefit of seeing her as a woman. This will give me a glimpse into who she really is. That could be good or bad. It will be enlightening.

13. I'm going to give Donald Trump the benefit of seeing him as a man. This will give me a glimpse into who he really is. That could be good or bad. It will also be enlightening.

14. Whatever is discovered, I will be at peace.

15. This rambling isn't going to be life changing. People love to be pissed. I get that.

16. But I will quietly remove myself from the room. I won't jump on the rampage. I'll be the soft voice. I'll be mocked. I'm used to it.

17. LOVE is the answer, whatever the question is, even - "Who am I going to vote for?"

It's Sunday. Another day to love. Happy Sunday.

Sunday Morning Ramblings: August 2016

1. I awoke this morning to the sound of my radio alarm tuned into the classical station. The song? Somewhere Over the Rainbow - instrumental.

2. "Someday I wish upon a star..."

3. Instrumental? Hmm. #lifechanger #dreamrecharge

4. What are your dreams? Are you doing anything, even one teeny thing, to make them come true? Or are we all just wishing...upon stars...and does that even work? I haven't tried it in a long time. I'm hoping for a clear night tonight. Anyone want to join me? #therearezillions #enoughforallofus

5. I work all day long. Every day...right up until I close my bedroom door at night to the relief and comfort of my bed. Some days I'm not cut out for this job. "...where trouble melts like lemon drops..."

6. My current bedside book is Infinite Possibilities. It's not all starry-eyed, dreamy, or spiritual. It's quite practical, as I am, even as a poet and writer and big time dreamer. I think when I became a mother I realized that practical would shape these beings a whole lot more than anything else. And now, I've begun throwing in some dreamy stuff...for them...just for fun. "...And the dreams that you dare to dream really do come true..."

7. So friends, it's time. Time to dream again. "...That's where you'll find me..."

8. Dream big. Don't be shy. And stop the complaining. That throws a wrench in things. "...birds fly over the rainbow..."

9. What are your thoughts? Are they pointing you in the direction of those dreams or are they yanking you backward? You were meant for bigger things...oh yes you were....see? "...there's a land that I've heard of..."

10. ...Skies are blue..." Let's take this show on the road.

11. I'm with you...all. the. Way. "...and wake up where the clouds are far behind me..."

12. You are a dreamer...for a reason. Those dreams need to come true for me and you and the folks whose dreams are dangling over their heads. Let's do this! "...If happy little bluebirds fly, beyond the rainbow..."

13. "Why, oh why...can't I?"

It's Sunday. Another day to love. Happy Sunday.

Being strong doesn't always mean you have to fight the battle. True strength is being adult enough to walk away from the nonsense with your head held high.

unknown

September

Sunday Morning Ramblings: September 2016

1. There was darkness a few days ago...in our freezer. The little appliance light bulb's life was done. Well, as these things go we kept opening the freezer door, several times a day, to the darkness, mentioning each time, aloud, "Oh that's right, we need to get a new light bulb." One day in all of our organized glory we trotted to HD and bought another little light bulb. EC put it in at some point and that was that. I never thought about the darkness again because there was light. Until, this morning, when I asked the Universe if there was a SMR (Sunday Morning Rambling) that needed to be written.

2. So we notice the darkness. It's uncomfortable. We become all squinty-eyed trying to search for...a bag of frozen corn...or maybe even our own life. Heads bent down, our bodies slightly hunched creating lower back pain. We don't like it, for the most part. It throws off our rhythm, the darkness. Because it is NOT who we are.

3. I'm gonna be so bold and say that WE ARE LIGHT. Oh come on, you know the difference. Walking in a dark room, you will pretty much always stub your toe. Pain. Excruciating. Yep, that's the darkness for you. Troublesome most of the time.

4. Now I'm not totally opposed to the darkness. Why just this morning, it was morning right? 7am. It was darker than usual outdoors. The 41 degree temperature made it chilly indoors. And I had a sweet smile on my face as I hobbled to the bathroom.

5. Natural darkness can be gorgeous all on its own. Whether Mother Nature and all her familiarity creates this or our own life shakes the darkness down. In those particular moments, where I get to release and cry and rock myself into comfort and summon my humanity, I've been healed and songs have been written.

6. However, the invitation of darkness is not the same. Now our darkness(es) are very different. Some are triggered by memory and loads of other things. Perhaps we've chosen some form of darkness and the consequences were really awful. Other times we are keenly aware that something dark will effect us deeply, so we turn away. Choosing darkness can have serious ill effects. We all know this, especially, each time we open that door.

7. I love the light. But I realized, because of my near blind rummage through the freezer last week, that my LOVE for the light comes out of the darkness.

8. That simple reminder that LIGHT is available to us. It's waiting for us.

9. When my boys were little EC taught them a song. They sang it everywhere singing could be had. "This little light of mine, I'm

gonna let it shine." A children's gospel song, yes. What I didn't know is that it was sung during the Civil Rights movement as a sort of anthem along with We Shall Overcome. The lyric, "I'm gonna let it shine" meant that we make the decision for ourselves.

10. Darkness is all around. Of course. But so is LIGHT.

11. There are gentle wisdom seekers all over this land who speak words of LIGHT. Choosing our words is very powerful. We can in one word, one word! bring the darkness. I've done it thousands of times. It's a real thing.

12. I've also chosen the word that illuminated our entire Universe here. That is also a real thing. One word that healed my family, calmed the entire day, changed my chemistry, quieted a doubt, and the list goes on.

13. Being a lover of the light in the midst of darkness is really NO CHALLENGE at all. However, it is a decision.

14. A decision we can make even as we rummage, hunched over, squinting our eyes to see what's on the shelf of our life.

15. Featherweight. No burden at all. Reaching for the light. It is merely a simple switch.

It's Sunday. Another day to love. Happy Sunday.

How wonderful it is that nobody need wait a single moment before starting to improve the world.

Anne Frank

October

Sunday Morning Ramblings: October 2016

1. What do you do with your POWER? You do realize you have power, right? Oh yes. We all do. While many of us may not walk in the circles of the rich and famous or big business or government there still remains an absolute - we all have power. Every day we choose, yes choose, to use our power - either in a productive way displaying to the Universe that we are contributing to our own little world. Or we acquiesce. There are varying degrees of our use scattered in between. However, we make a decision as to what to do with our power...everyday.

2. Older siblings wield their power over younger siblings. Younger siblings then search for something to use their power over. It appears to be an inherent piece of our humanity.

3. Nature has power. If there is a decision making process in its use of power I've yet to discover that. However, there is definitely power in all forms of nature. Most think of storms when power and nature are side by side. Yet, the power of a rose bloom on a spring day has quite literally been so powerful that I've wept. Nature's power for light and life are so strong, so joined, that in the cracks there appears a bloom.

4. We were offered a little bit of power *at the building* down the street - the one masquerading as a loving entity of the maker of

the Universe. We didn't want it...as in yuk, puke! We felt defiled. They offered again. We refused. And again. No, was our final answer...forever. Now, don't go thinking, "How enlightened they are for seeing through that" - we still struggled with the issue of our power. We stayed in a place where the abuse of power was so rampant it has now altered generations...not for the good. But that's not my story. It's theirs. And just like I chose to leave.. they can also do the same. Power.

5. I see power as being available like a tangible offering. "Here is your power. Sitting right over there. Go pick it up." What will you do with it? Power.

6. The abuse of power runs wild. We read about it. We listen to it in the news. We see it...everywhere. It's been going on for like say...since the Universe began. Power.

7. Can those who abuse power change? I would like to say YES. It's not as popular to do. It requires great introspection. An awakening has to occur. However, if power is all you desire, then good luck. You won't be changing any time soon.

8. Is having power altogether a bad thing? The power to paint my face with make-up or color my hair seems pretty benign. When I wield my power with my children it takes 7 minutes for Karma to have her say. I'm grateful. I don't want to be the most powerful "mother" in the house.

9. So what do we do with all this power we have available? Do we use it for the good of humanity? Do we free people with our words, our actions? Or do we do our best to make sure

everyone's light stays dim because we won't let our bright light shine?

10. It's a touchy thing...this power. Use it for good? Or not. Help people grow? Or not. Change our world for the better? Or not.

11. Power can be in the form of a whining rant as well. I used to whine and rant. I can't tolerate that anymore. Not because I sit in judgment of the whiner, but because I know better and the person ranting is SO MUCH MORE THAN THAT. Whether I know them personally or not.

12. So power and light are comrades. They keep each other in check. If there's barely any light in the room, good chance your power has been wielded for something other than the best of intentions.

13. We have the power to make people feel. It's daunting. I've ruined an entire moment in time by wielding my power for something other than the light.

14. I keep hoping everyone becomes enlightened in their use of their personal power. It won't happen. But I'll keep hoping.

15. Power.

It's Sunday Another day to love Happy Sunday.

Sunday Morning Ramblings: October 2016

1. This may be a doozy, folks. Hold on.

2. Remember it's a rambling. I never know what is going to be written until I begin typing.

3. If someone left a small pile of garbage in your way, would you continually kick it around the room or take 2 seconds to bend down and put it where it belongs? Remember our lives were never made for other people's trash.

4. The Universe will support our decisions, whatever they may be. Free will. We can convince our minds of anything. Our physical bodies may even crumble. Our spirit, however, will sit and wait, toe tapping, for lifetimes. #getwithyourspirit

5. Being brave only costs a little. It's just our lives we're talking about. #realmetaphor

6. "Oh, I'll just do it myself." And the Earth and the Wind smiled at each other. The Sun did not move.

7. Let's take some time to think about the paths we traverse. #grabsomegoodshoes

8. I call *them*, The Evils, now. They threaten people. *They* separate families. *They* rob them of their money. *They* play with people's minds. *They* are constantly lifting others up to then tear

them down. *They* work them until they are broken. And *they* call *themselves* the "elite of God." We are now clear which god they serve. And *they* don't pay taxes. How 'bout that? Whoa.

9. It's heartbreaking, especially to me. I'm a lover. I love easily and willingly without expectation. It's my favorite and most honest part of my soul, to love others. I've been hurt many times for loving others. Bullies see Lovers as weak. But Love is and forever will be the strongest. The bully will do harm and then lose. Always. There's never a win for the bully. Did you read that? "Never a win for the bully." The Lover, however, does not lose a single thing. #pickyourselfupandmoveon

10. The other day I grabbed a metaphorical stick and drew a line in the sand. I realized I didn't need the wall anymore. The line was enough.

11. When I meet with folks who are trying to survive a cult I am reminded just how powerful the mind is - the entanglement so knotted that the left and right brains are in fisticuffs. And yet, that brain is in their head not only trying to keep them alive, but trying to give them a beautiful life.

12. The other day, Intuition sat down and had a conversation with Logic. They realized they were more alike than they thought. #brainprofundity

13. Peace is beautiful.

14. Get to know yourself, your true self - not the self you've been told you are - the Self, with the uppercase "S" - the one that is like none other. #truebeauties

15. I love people. I hope for people. I pray for people. People are stunning in their true essence. I thank the Universe/God for giving me a heart that sees. #grateful

It's Sunday. Another day to love. Happy Sunday.

There is only one way to avoid criticism.
Do nothing. Say nothing and Be nothing.

Aristotle

December

Sunday Morning Ramblings: December 2016

1. I know. It's been a while.

2. Peace on Earth? First, let me ask, as an individual do you have peace-peace that is available right now, this moment? If not, then let's stop the arrogant request that peace be on Earth. #itisallaboutyou

3. I believe in Evolution. Yet, there is quite a load of evidence that it is NOT for everyone. #evolve

4. Hate and rage of any kind makes one a master of? #slave

5. If we could simply let it be, I wonder what would happen? #love? #joy? #peace?

6. There's a line in a yet-to-be famous song, "Enlighten Your Load." #glorystory #freetofindpearls #bebrave

7. The broader view allows - did you see that - ALLOWS us to change our focus. #itisaGIFT #seemore

8. I write for myself. #haveNOTmasteredmuch

9. I was asked to sing Leonard Cohen's Hallelujah. I went to the other room and cried. #honored

10. My studio is starting to take shape. Translation: Yesterday, I spent time in there walking around, taking notice of the light,

feeling the carpet with my toes, looking out the windows, studying the space. #writer #creator

11. I am an inspector of words. #watchwhatissaid #wordshavepower

12. These are ramblings.

13. The ground outside is white. I am happy. #winter #Xskiing #hiking #scarves #funkyhats

14. Is enough enough?

15. Make a space in your heart today, for you.

It's Sunday. Another day to love. Happy Sunday.

2017

Notice the people who are happy for your happiness and sad for your sadness. They are the ones who deserve special places in your heart.

unknown

January

Sunday Morning Ramblings: January 2017

1. Be careful of groups.

2. I tried to belong to *a group* for about 15 years. It was oppressive, controlling, demanding, a form of human trafficking, exhausting, taking my time and money for its own egotistical and tyrannical purposes. The group NEVER cares for the individual. EVER.

3. The disgusting thing about groups is they become another religion. Religions oppress. Period. People are never truly free within the confines of the group. It's unnatural.

4. I "march" everyday against groups and religion, lies and false ideologies, global atrocities, and FOR human rights, dignity, fairness by living my life, loving my family and friends, being me, teaching my sons, writing POETRY and words, creating a loving environment not only in my home but in my HEART. It is daunting at times, this mantle I carry. Sometimes I kick and scream, make a mess of things. But one thing I know without a doubt - NO ONE will EVER be in CHARGE of how I DESIGN MY LIFE. The LEADER is me. I know everything about her. I've come to trust her.

5. Know who your leader is. Find everything out about him/her if you feel the need to be led. If you stand behind or with someone make sure you completely understand what THEY stand for. Whatever we attach ourselves to is what we become. Or, what we come to HATE.

6. The ego feels the need to march. The heart simply knows where the march is every single moment. It is within.

7. Trusting our hearts is no easy task. Yet, it remains the ONLY way to finding OUR PERSONAL TRUTH. And sometimes that begins by marching with a group or attaching ourselves to one...until...

8. There is great strength in finding out the TRUTH. It's quite messy and uncomfortable. But keep looking at it. After a while it becomes the most perfect creation your eyes have ever delighted in. And you become completely and wholly UNAFRAID.

9. Groups are prison.

10. They ALL begin with a false sense of LOVE and JOY and PERFECTION. A romance. Until someone leaves their smelly socks on the floor. Or thousands of posters strewn about on the streets for the cities to clean up. Oy.

11. If you're going to be the leader of a group at least put together a clean up crew. Not right.

12. Ladies, no one in the United States of America has control over your vagina unless you hand it over to them. Period. Be careful who you give it to.

13. Who's fighting for the truly oppressed women in other countries who have NO RIGHTS AT ALL? I'll have to look into that.

14. Remember I mentioned a few weeks ago that if you don't know me I'm the one in the room who is always full of hope? I was that woman yesterday as I watched women all over the world march. I HOPED for them. I wished for them a deeper understanding into who they are as individuals.

15. Because I am a woman? No. Because whatever cause someone feels passionate about I pray they move in the direction, solely and soul-y, to that purpose. Change from within being their directive.

16. Not all women were invited. Some were asked to leave.

17. Be careful of groups. Trust me on this one.

It's Sunday. Another day to love. Happy Sunday

Perhaps I am stronger than I think.

Thomas Merton

February

Sunday Morning Ramblings: February 2017

1. Deep down we already know the truth.

2. So what it is the truth?

3. Perhaps that we're all BLOODY TERRIFIED?

4. Terrified that our beliefs won't be the "right" ones?

5. Terrified that NO one will listen and we won't EVER be heard?

6. Terrified that the group we identify with isn't the "correct" group?

7. Terrified that EVERYTHING will be stripped away from us in a moment?

8. Terrified that we WON'T get IT right...whatever IT is?

9. Or perhaps the truth is more sleepy, lying dormant and if IT comes out we'll be eaten alive by THAT ROARING LION?

10. And shaking, we won't LOOK right to the GROUP or the PERSON WHO SITS ON THE THRONE WE'VE SELECTIVELY PUT THEM ON?

11. Perhaps our truth is that WE DON'T HAVE A FLIPPIN CLUE ABOUT ANYTHING and we don't want to be found out?

12. Perhaps our truth is a MONSTER?

13. A MONSTER, with a name, a face, a vestment, a suit, a hat, a stick, reeking of booze or perfume, cologne, smiling?

14. And we WILL do anything, say ANYTHING to get away from that LIE to create OUR OWN TRUTH to be SAFE?

15. We will CLING like the frightened child that we ARE to anyone who will HOLD us...even if their TRUTH is not completely OURS.

16. Underneath all the tidy piles of life, behind all the closet doors, in between the layers of fabric and all the scars is a TRUTH that was molded from someone else's LIE.

17. It's not YOUR truth.

18. It's NOT their truth.

19. Our TRUTH is not where wrath or protest shouts.

20. Our TRUTH is deep; deep down. MINE. YOURS.

21. Whatever our TRUTHS, they must be uncovered, TRUTH MUST be revealed.

22. In this moment in time, in life and in history OUR TRUTHS will not all be aligned, if ever.

23. If I am to remain in the TRUTH, I must ALLOW you YOUR TRUTH. Otherwise I will discount MINE.

24. Dig deep. We MUST. There is simply NO other way for us to peacefully co-habitate and quite possibly LOVE each other, exactly and wholly, in our broken pieces, each one of us, together.

It's Sunday. Another day to love. Happy Sunday.

Sunday Morning Ramblings: February 2017

1. Hi ya'll. I really love saying that.

2. I've met some new friends who are supporting our President. It's nice to meet some folks who are not mad at everybody or rage at the other side. That tires me out...utterly and completely. We don't all agree with everything either. It's how it used to be...when disagreeing was simply another person's perspective based on their life's experiences. Can we ALL agree that we have different life experiences? I hope so. Because I love you all. That never wavers.

3. If you remember correctly, I don't jump on hate bandwagons EVER. If I had a religion, it would be against that. #lovefirst

4. Love is like silk - smooth, shimmery, requiring delicate care. Let's remember this.

5. Love is also like denim - sturdy, rugged, withstanding frays, holes, tears. Let's remember this, too.

6. I haven't talked about my studio loft in a while. It was completed 3 months after the planned project finish date. Isn't that fun? Not really. But like so many late arrivals or past deadlines, once the goods arrive in all their splendor we no longer whine about the delay. #didIjustwhine

7. The space, so far, has morphed into my writing loft (using my FIL's antique desk - story coming soon), my sewing and fabric sculpture lab, my mini-dance studio, my prayer & meditation room and my yoga pad. I haven't begun painting in there yet. I'm waiting to find the perfect drafting table. Oh, the mere mention of that THRILLS MY SOUL! #canvasAwaits

8. Last night, EC and the boys participated in a fundraising BB event. The spirit of these folks was so beautiful! I love people!

9. While taking Liza, our lab/Doberman mix dear-hearted girl dog for a walk yesterday, earbuds in, listening to Florence and the Machine, I may have been singing out loud. I was definitely singing out loud. Our neighbors were wearing the BIGGEST smiles as I passed by their driveway. I didn't dwell on their interpretation. Sometimes it's better not to know. #keepwalkin!

10. Being a multi-creative being has its woes. I'm working on decorating my studio, while I'm writing songs, finishing fabric projects, creating a business, revamping my website, designing t-shirts, sketching my next paintings, re-designing my clothes, drawing new landscape projects, creating a women's group,

piecing together the poetry and artwork for 2 books and finishing up my novel...seriously the list goes on...throw in home school & college, basketball, 2 teenagers, 1 husband, working out, feeding everyone, cleaning the house, keeping up with the mountains of laundry, maintaining relationships with friends and family and all of a sudden I realize…
I'M WONDER WOMAN!!!
#woesGONE #gettingsomebracelets

11. These are ramblings.

12. Be with people who support life. It'll keep you living.

13. I love coffee. No seriously, I LOVE it.

14. I wish my mom and dad were healthy and could enjoy life and be a part of mine. #sad

15. I love people, whatever state they're in. #heartties

16. So grateful for my guy - who rocks my world - shaking the loose dirt, settling the giant boulders and revealing to me that flowers bloom even in the cracks and crevasses. #seektheLIGHT

It's Sunday. Another day to love. Happy Sunday.

All that matters is my relationship to you.

Van Morrison

Sunday Morning Ramblings: March 2017

1. I still love people.

2. I've been to hell.

3. I came back.

4. Heaven is on earth.

5. So is hell.

6. But don't let any of it get you down.

7. Unless you want to be down, of course.

8. People are flawed.

9. People are miracles.

10. People are people. #seriously #flawed #miracles

11. Everyday choose love.

12. Or choose hate. It IS up to you.

13. I'm still in love, with love.

14. We are never alone, if we acknowledge our true self within us. #within

15. There's a shift happening. No, not that one. You must dig deep inside your soul's eyes to see it, feel it, know it. Test: You'll know it, if it doesn't make you afraid.

16. The Lovers are finding each other. #happy

17. Keep searching.

18. Never. Give. Up.

It's Sunday. Another day to love. Happy Sunday.

Sunday Morning Ramblings: March 2017

1. The Revelation of Love. How 'bout that instead of all this other nonsense?

2. When does the revelation come? When love occupies the space completely and wholly. All others keep walkin'.

3. Revelations are a revealing, a telling, an awareness, a dawning, an uncovering of some idea/fact/truth that was

otherwise hidden or concealed. Revelations are provocations of the mind, the heart, or the spirit leading one toward abundant living and true love.

4. A revelation may happen at any moment. The revelation is a constant and the receiver may or may not be good. It simply does not matter. The revelation, once available, remains open, laying out the possibility for good, for better choices, better understanding for only those who choose this way of thinking, living. The revelation simply is. It is never a respecter of persons. Is the light? We all see the light in a room, correct?

5. A revelation parts seas. Yes. It also parts ways. It changes dimensions, dynamics, physics, friendships, relationships, and the course of history on an individual plane and a global one.

6. Who wants a revelation?

7. Do we want to know, to understand, to be complete?

8. If we do, be prepared for a dawning. It will come. Keep in mind we may not care for it. But understand it will
always
ALWAYS
ALWAYS
offer us the highest and most generous service to our life.

9. The revelation is for you. The revelation is for our better self, our higher self. Never anything else. Yet, we get the daunting task of making the choice whether it frees us from bondage or not. The choice is ours.

10. If we dream a gorgeous life, a beautiful existence, then we must be willing to accept and trust the revelations that wake us up. We MUST be unafraid. The revelation may shake us. It will NEVER destroy us.

11. Revelations keep us on our OUR path. The straight and narrow only appear to be divergent because we do not trust the truth...yet. Our paths are perfect when we trust.

12. Revelations remind us of who we have the capacity to become. Our natural state of being is within the revelation.

13. I love you.

14. These are ramblings.

It's Sunday. Another day to love. Happy Sunday

An unexamined life is not worth living.

Socrates

April

Sunday Morning Ramblings: April 2017

1. I've come to the conclusion that I have friends in this entire Universe. When the stars call out my name, I love them all. #lovingpeople #kindredspirits

2. It is the soul that meets and greets its loves, and hangs on with such delicacy, like the silkworm weaver. #soul #friends

3. If being practical were "en vogue" where would I go, who would I be? What sort of life would I live? #creator

4. Is it the responsibility of the responsible to be responsible for the irresponsible? I wonder. #toughquestion

5. Picking up the pieces and creating a life is one thing. Picking up the pieces and scattering them into the wind can be the most beautiful thing. Ever. #letitgo

6. I am the product of my thinking. Or the bagel I just ate. #wonder

7. I. must. look. up. #theUNlimitedSKYbeckons

8. Remember that deep breath? It can save your life. #breathe

9. It is okay to accept what is...because, really, we are the only ones who need to change. #ouch

10. Poetry is my song, sung from the depths of an unaware, sleeping soul, lying dormant awaiting the arrival of her royal garments and crown. #sing #write

11. The tower is in our mind; as is the power. #freeorcaptive

12. Everything is hard.

13. Everything is easy.

14. Time didn't stand still this morning. #sprung

15. There is goodness all around. If you don't believe it, you are right. #believe

16. I don't always take the time. I prefer to give it. #lessons #remember

17. This rambling may never end... #ha

It's Sunday Another day to love. Happy Sunday

Sunday Morning Ramblings: April 2017

1. So, we are expected to believe in magic.

2. Totally cool. I love magic.

3. I've experienced many magical things so far in this life.

4. Magic cannot be explained.

5. If a magician appears (lol) and starts performing "magic" this is not real magic. We must understand the difference.

6. Magic is magic. Magicians who do magic are not actually making magic. They are playing with our brain...and sometimes our heart...but most definitely our reality.

7. To witness a truly magical experience we must be here; here, as in the present. Magic happens no matter what. Whether we are present or not. It happens all day and all night long. Remember to witness it we must be present. Our lack of presence never alters the magical. There are no rules or plans or designs for magic to happen. (remember that would NOT be magic - it would be manipulation)

8. All sorts of books have been written about the subject. People have designed full blown religions based on words and accounts of magical happenings. This is also not real magic.

9. Magic happens to anyone, whether we have a trusty belief system or not.

10. Magic is not a story.

11. Magic is actually real. It never needs to be proven. It happens in the moment...when we are present. That moment can last for eternity in our memory or possibly in our DNA but it can never be duplicated. If we try, we just became a magician or a priest or a god and that makes it defunct.

12. If we've ever experienced magic we may have cheapened it by labeling it something. However, enormous volumes of poetry have been trying to explain magic for centuries. Holy books have been written. Those books are even worshiped because of

the magic in them. And yet, in the present is where the magic is. Never the past. Even if we can remember it. And even if we've read about it.

13. However, magic is so very real. It definitely can be experienced in the future; as long as we are present once the future arrives. That would then make it the present. However, we remain hopeful for magic again sometime soon, regardless. The more present we become, the more magic we experience.

14. Magic exists. Do you know how I know this? Because I can not, nor will I ever be able to explain love.

15. Love is magic.

It's Sunday Another day to love Happy Sunday

Everything that is really great and inspiring is created by the individual who can labor in freedom.

Albert Einstein

may

Sunday Morning Ramblings: Mother's Day 2017

1. I'm a mother. #truth

2. I never wanted to be a mother. #anothertruth

3. ...as in dreamed about it or anything of the sort. I wanted freedom and complete dominion over my life. lol

4. It's true. #NoLie

5. So when I met this guy a while back, I thought, "Maybe I could be a mother with him." #Icanbe #differentstory

6. He'd be a good father and a cool guy to hang out with for the next thousand years or so, while I'm a mother. #funtimes

7. And let me tell you, motherhood lasts that long. If not, longer. #longer

8. This gig is forever. #forever

9. It doesn't end at any point. #nope #never

10. I'm glad I chose it. There are days, of course. But days fade, in time. #fade

11. The essence is what remains. #true

12. In the beginning, my heart kept them alive. Today, it's still beating for them. #heart

13. This all consuming life I now live for other people is not a possession,

a charm,

a reward,

a trophy or accomplishment for display.

It is a gift.

To call it anything else would diminish its worth.

14. To all the mothers out there whose heart beats are keeping their children alive, I thank you. #grateful #youarethemostbeautifulcreaturesontheplanet

Happy Mother's Day

It's Sunday Another day to love Happy Sunday

The genius is the one who is most like himself.

Thelonious Monk

June

Sunday Morning Ramblings: June 2017

1. I'm a lover...of love. I love love so much. I dare myself daily to get to love. In this beguiling conquest I find that without notice Love's arrow touches me. #grateful #usuallyfromanunexpectedsource

2. I love to explore energy. Living with three science guys I've come to understand Quantum Physics, a bit. Let me rephrase that: There have been many dinner table discussions about it. Please don't ask me to explain the science. I understand things best with my heart. If my heart gains the wisdom that is all I require. So consider the energy of the folks in the room. Sometimes a push and the other a pull. We all sense it, feel it. Not all of us know what to do with these two forms of energy. So let me ask, "How long are they allowed to remain in that state?" #choices #power #altertheenergy #heartbrain

3. Many people can remain in an inner push/pull for the entirety of their lives. #uncomfortableself

4. My astrological sign is mutable. I love knowing that about myself. In this understanding I see the strength in the ability to bend and change. For years I judged myself harshly. #nomorejudgment #altertheenergy

5. Oh and please, stop judging yourself. Unless, of course you need to alter the energy. Then do that. #thankyou

6. Many people can remain with another in a push/pull time and space for the entirety of their lives. #uncomfortableness

7. I cleaned out my closet. #yep

8. These are ramblings.

9. If we take more than we give, what do we actually get?

10. EC told me the other day, as I cried on his shoulder for the 9,845,324,006th time, "The true artist emerges from experience and great suffering." The metamorphosis, if you will. Pushing my way out of the chrysalis. Do we ever arrive? #wondering

11. Some people dream about far off lands. *hand raised

12. And some people dream of officiating at weddings. *hand raised waving One more step for me in the ordination process of being an Officiating Minister. #soexcited #IloveLOVE #weddings

13. Be who YOU are - not an imitation of who some folks think you should be. But the YOU that claws at the inner skin of that cocoon, pekks out now and again. The one who dreams secret dreams and sees beautiful realities with YOU sitting in them, right in the midst. You don't need to leave your people to be

YOU. Begin on a Wednesday, after an 8 hour day, or a Saturday morning with the glistening dew. A little step is always and forever a step forward. #thankyou #IloveYOU

14. Being afraid is part of everything. "Fear, come on over and sit down with me. I won't run from you anymore." #love #art

15. When EC and I married, I thought I was the least likely to marry ever in the history of ever and forever. I proved myself wrong. #gettoLOVE #abeguilingconquest ;)

16. My hope for all of you, my lovely friends, is that YOU are YOU today. Yes, with the same tribe you woke up with, the same hair and body shape, the same dwelling place. Because LOVE is right here. Right now. But you do need to find it. #keepsearching

It's Sunday. Another day to love. Happy Sunday.

Sunday Morning Ramblings: June 2017

1. Father's Day. This is a tough one for me. My dad is still here. But he's gone. Living another life. Without me.

2. Father's Day. This is a tough one for me. My FIL is gone. I wish he was still here. Living with us. And our sons.

3. Father's Day. This is a miracle for me. My husband is the father of our sons. Living a wild and gorgeous life. With us.

4. I can be both gratefully happy while feeling deeply sad.

5. Tangerine is a tasty fruit. Just not sure it should be the color of my art studio door. #livingonthewildside #studioloft #EC #photoswillbeposted #HomeDepot #choosingpaintcolorstoday I'm *not* calling it ORANGE. lol

6. This weekend is party central. Grad parties. Wedding parties. I love people.

7. At one of the grad parties I was reminded of the goodness of souls. #getoutofyourself #payattention #listentoanotherspeak

8. There is goodness all around. #keepourheartsopen

9. Every shower I take, songs dangle in the air above me. I have to ask them to please wait...will they wait...I hope they wait...

10. The other day in all the transformation and creative work going on in my studio, I found a note stuck to my desk. "I love you Mom." #tears #relief #blessed

11. I was reminded that, as an Ordained Minister, I will be in many wedding photos. #neverthoughtofthat #lovebeingthemotivator #newwardrobe

12. When I have a free moment I watch a Turkish television series.

13. I miss my bike. She's teal. Time to get her out and show her the town.

14. I love my friends; those with wheels and without.

15. Party in July at my house. #missmyfriends #gettingthroughtheschoolyear

16. If you don't have a father, or have never experienced the love of a father please know I'm carrying YOU in particular with me today. #tenderness
Happy Father's Day

It's Sunday. Another day to love. Happy Sunday

We can easily forgive a child who is afraid of the dark; the real tragedy of life is when men are afraid of the light.

Plato

July

Sunday Morning Ramblings: July 2017

1. If in all things we can get to love, I believe this to be the bravest part of life and living. #nomatterwhat

2. Sometimes getting to love is an action or word or silent moment, apart and separate from anyone else.

3. "A strong man is the hottest thing on the freakin planet," said an honest woman. #yesALLhonestwomen

4. Take care. #please

5. Being aware of others is a gift. Some of us haven't opened that box yet in life. When we do...such a gift...to ourselves and everyone around us. #aware

6. My life so far has been full of holes, empty holes, damages seemingly irreparable...and yet, there remains this gorgeous fascination with filling these cavernous craters with love. #whatremains #choices #loss

7. And...I am never empty. #full

8. If we run away, we will always have ourselves. There is good in this. However, who and what we leave behind must be greater than ourselves, if we are to stay. If we find that is not the case, then we must not run away, but let it go like blowing the little feathers off the dandelion. And make a wish. #gentleliving

9. Sleep is my love.

10. These are ramblings.

11. Dance if you can.

12. We don't know everyone nor do we understand everyone's actions/words/behaviors. Let's realize this and simply let people be.

13. I've removed all hate & negativity from my Facebook feed. It does a body good; a mind and spirit, too.

14. Tomorrow is a special day in my life. Me and my guy. #love

15. Let some stuff go wrong/right/perfect/haphazard/crazy. Stop trying to control it ALL. It'll be a reminder that what you have right in front of you is absolute perfection or not. But at least you will be available to see it. #handsoff #perspective #adjustment

16. I love a gentle breeze.

It's Sunday Another day to love. Happy Sunday

Sunday Morning Ramblings: July 2017

1. So, I wonder if the dream last night of me swimming - in my clothing - on and around rocks and tree branches - to locate a centipede for a museum collection had anything to do with my third eye noticing a giant black spider crawling on the ceiling above my bed while I slept. Ahh! Lord, help me! #wakingUPearlyisagoodthing

2. What does your 3rd eye notice when your other eyes can't see? #payattention

3. Lime water does a body good.

4. Ramblings...

5. I planked before I went to bed last night. #popcorn #chocolatecoveredcherries However, I did eat an apple at yesterday's music gig. #wasthatsomesortofconfession

6. How do we know how to do this life? It's a phenomenon. Truly. #youwillNEVERerrorifyouLOVE

7. At times we misunderstand the feeling of "being stuck" with "it's time to slow down" or "it's time to move." Coming to an abrupt halt means there's a fork in the road; which way do we choose? Or perhaps it's a dead end. Either way. We can choose

a different path, one that others have paved already or begin to bushwhack our own. #theybothtakeusplaces

8. My 35th high school reunion was last night. I wasn't available to attend. However, as the Universe would have it, my husband and I and our sons were supporting a family whose beautiful young daughter left this earth too early. She attended the same school, as her parents, her family and I did. Her grandfather was our superintendent during my junior and senior years. #connected #beautifulevent #lifeaffirming

9. The world is a dot - a teeny, tiny dot and here we are all crammed on it living much closer in space and time and heart than we realize.

10. My sons jammed out some serious rock and roll yesterday. #proudmomma #proudpoppa #freedom #art #music #heartfeltcause

11. Having true friends is the most beautiful creation in this life. We walk on in the wilderness or through the valleys or up mountain paths to eventually come to a breath-taking vista, or a rare wild flower in and among the greens. Our senses come alive with relief, reunion and rejuvenation and restoration. We have found one another here at this time, in this moment. This rare joining, we have no power in creating. Our hearts and spirits dance. It is truly a gift. #wefoundeachother

12. I'm working on 3 paintings this week. One is a gift. The other two are also. I don't know what they will look like or what

they are about yet or even who they belong to. As soon as I do, I'll share. #inspiration #prayer #canvas

13. Pink is my color of choice lately. I'm drawn to it. It heals me then lifts my spirit. #calm #tranquil #affectionate

14. Painting is my song.

15. I love to sing.

It's Sunday. Another day to love. Happy Sunday.

Sunday Morning Ramblings: July 2017

1. So I sit down to write something meaningful. First I'll check my email. Class schedules are out! Excitement exudes! #school #teacher #learning #didImentionexcitement

2. I've been a teacher for nearly 17 years. #loveit #homeschool #lifeschool #gentlemen #care #kindness

3. EC teaches them how to be men. And athletes. And wild survivalists. And musicians. And science guys. And astronomers. Historians. And soldiers in the army of life as well as gentlemen. #Imarriedajewel

4. I teach them that, "YES! In fact it does matter that you pick up your socks, clean off the table and say, thank you!" #moms

5. Life is busier with teenagers in the house. Busier than babies. Busier than toddlers. #howcanthatbepossible

6. My hope is that we've done a good job. Because by now, other than some life skills, they're pretty much nurtured to the max.

7. I'm so grateful I chose to become a mom. It's my favorite job in all the land. It's the most difficult job - so much is on the line. And I haven't earned a single dime doing it. #canweputapriceonraisingupalife

8. I'm still attending the "School of Hard Knocks." #lifelongstudent

9. My boys are both in high school now. Today, they may be meeting some friends of mine from when I was in high school. #surreal

10. Is all giving sacrificial? Should it be? Does it matter? Sometimes? #ponderings

11. I took a nap like nobody's business yesterday. #rewardsforbeingaMom

12. I've always napped. I love napping. #noTypeAhere #nappedinschool #nappedincollege #nappedinNYC #alwaysanapper #proudnapper #thenmyeveningsROCK

13. It's so much easier to love people. Can we get on that bandwagon? #nojudgments #noagendas #nopointingfingers #noholierthanThourules #allthatisNONSENSE

14. My studio is up and running. I love it so much. A couple weeks ago it was a B&B for a friend. It's a place of deep conversation and counsel. It's a safe-haven for those special chats with my sons. It's my yoga studio, my writing studio, my nature studio, my painting studio, my sanctuary. It is a place where I'll meet couples to go over the details of their weddings. It is where my books are finished and put together. It is where I sit and ramble. It is where I can fully express my soul. It is where I am free to find my pearls - and gently study them, close to my heart, laying them on velvet cloths, giving them a shine. #grateful #artistry

15. EC is washing pans in the kitchen. I hear the clanging. Or maybe he's using his culinary skills to make breakfast. Either one makes me smile. #simpleliving

16. Tomorrow I see MY GIRLFRIENDS from high school!!! WOOHOO!

It's Sunday. Another day to love. Happy Sunday.

Sunday Morning Ramblings: July 2017

1. I've got a few questions.

2. If an immoral person does a good deed does that deed remain good?

3. If an immoral organization helps people is that true help?

4. How can we be sure someone or some organization has a clean heart or integrity?

5. If a person or organization has very little integrity but offers help should we take it?

6. Who's keeping score?

7. What is love?

8. If tearing down walls can make us feel more vulnerable in an open space, what does putting walls up do...exactly?

9. Some love nooks and crannies, some wide open spaces. Which one is best?

10. I try not to cross the line. But I still do. Doesn't that mean I've finished the race? Maybe even winning it? Or does it?

11. Have you ever lived in another person's skin?

12. Decisions and choices, reactions and responses. Do they come from inside or outside the skin? Or both?

13. The simple gesture of gently wrapping one's arm around another, drawing them in just a little bit closer to the group can be an act of inclusion far superior than any other.

14. I love people...even the flawed ones..even those who failed me...even those who failed you. Why? Because inside every person's skin is a beating heart whose broken pieces have a grip so fierce, clinging to a thousand hurts, keeping them alive. Just like me. Just like you.

It's Sunday. Another day to love. Happy Sunday.

Driven by the forces of love, the fragments of the world seek each
other so that the world may come to being.

Pierre Teilhard de Chardin

August

Sunday Morning Ramblings: August 2017

1. Let's collect so much joy that our wounds heal, our hearts mend, our minds find peace.

2. Clearly it is NOT time that heals everything.

3. It is love. Only love; careful love that delicately places a soft dressing on the wound.

4. We must allow the air to get in.

5. Yes, the crust eventually falls away; there remains a scar, perhaps, making this area stronger, firmer reminding us we've made it through.

6. Memories can take us back to *that place*. Remember to bring your heart with you when you visit.

7. Or is it that joy, happiness, peace, and contentment are so light, storing them is nearly impossible? If so, then let us be so full, we are carried away.

8. I'm a writer. I can share your pain along with mine like comrades in a battle. We do this together. My pen, my arrow… for you.

9. Let me write your song. I will sing it from the mountain peak and hold the note with a deep, abiding breath...for you.

10. I'm a peacemaker. A diplomat. My inner-sight is multi-dimensional...for you.

11. Tearing pieces into bits will eventually create dust. One exhalation...for you, my love.

12. When I wear my heart on my sleeve, I am cradling yours with my other hand.

13. It is still beating...

14. Can we be so honest with ourselves that as the gates crumble and the walls topple, we stand long enough to see the garden?

15. If we run, we remain. Best to stand.

It's Sunday. Another day to love. Happy Sunday

Sunday Morning Ramblings: August 2017

1. Sometimes I have other things to do. You too?

2. I think I can, I think I can, I think I can...

3. Do we believe in love and then never allow it to conquer anything?

4. I am more of a woman today than I've ever been in my entire life. And I've got to say it's really rad!

5. My book has taken another turn. Holy Moly! How in the world am I gonna do this? You know, write it how Inspiration just delivered it? If there is a word organizer Angel available, could someone please send him/her to me for assistance? Thanks.

6. School is fast approaching and all I can think of is my crockpot.

7. I need help...with everything. But I hardly ever ask.

8. Our 13yo is playing his banjo at a festival today. #proudmommamoment #determined

9. Putting together my family tree. Just learned I am French and very Irish. Oh the places we will go!!!!! #hungarian #scottish #czech #austrian #russian #gypsy

10. I still miss my dad.

11. Ramblings...

12. Timing is everything, I've heard and said many a thousand times. It's the waiting that gets me.

13. I still believe that love wins in the end. I also believe it wins in the beginning and middle too, as well as in the corners and nooks, crevasses and wrinkles, tears and bends, folds and crumbles. It's in the seen and unseen. It rides a river, and is challenged by an eddy. It jumps off cliffs and hang glides into peaceful grasses. Love makes a way. Love carries us, delivers us, pushes us. Love helps us grow, flourish, become. If we can offer love to another, in a moment in time, its effects alter the Universe. The stars take notice. The moon brighter, your heartbeat stronger. It will literally change you and everything around you.

14. I wish I could erase all the ill I've caused others. One big eraser, like I used to mime for my sons when they were little and we ALL woke up on the wrong side of the bed. I'd grab that "eraser" and declare, "Everyone, back to bed. We're gonna erase this morning and start a new one." My arms swinging in the air in a wide swooping motion. They'd giggle and crawl back into bed, squinting eyes, pretending to be asleep. "Ok, Good morning boys!" They'd jump from their beds and wiggle out their doors laughing. And I'd tilt my head toward Heaven, with tears in my eyes and whisper, "Thank you."

15. Second chances are available. They're plentiful. And free.

It's Sunday. Another day to love. Happy Sunday.

Sunday Morning Ramblings: August 2017

1. Our heightened emotions only allow our perspectives to be those sitting on a pinhead looking at life through a pinhole. #stayclear

2. I believe I may have heard one hand clapping. #wakeup

3. I tried to focus on being just one thing...and then...oh never mind. #multidimensionalMe

4. My older brother is the best. The Best. As in, THE BEST. #blessedwehavecomethisfartogether (he'll notice the word - fart - in that hashtag)

5. On my morning walk, as I passed the lovely homes with the lovely people inside, listening to the sounds of the natural morning, a voice caught my attention. She was praying out loud, with a heavenly force, "In Jesus name!" That single phrase brought back a flood of memories - some really beautiful - of a congregation of heartfelt souls gathering together for one wholly and holy purpose. And yet, I felt only the heart of one soul today. I silently thanked her. #prayingpeoplearecool #beliefsystemsarejustthat #stopthinkingyouhavethemarketcorneredonyours

6. Words are powerful. The heart more powerful. And the soul? Baby, look out! If you desire a change, a real change, I highly

recommend face down in the dirt. That's the only place we truly grow from....yep. #BeBrave #thisisnotaboutaReligion

7. I love you.

8. Sometimes I dream of seeing everyone's soul first, meeting them in that perfect dimension. And then I set out to do just that...every....single...day. #lovesdoesGoodStuff

9. I refuse to jam along with the media or the right or the left. They will never sing MY song. Ever.

10. Don't forget there is more love around than anything else. And the cup never empties. And sometimes, you have to be the one who fills it up. #getbusy

11. I volunteer every.single.day. Can I get an AMEN from all the moms? #muchLoveandStrengthtoYouGirlFriends

12. When a husband answers for his wife with pause and hesitation as her joy is ignited, to then be snuffed out...well...I have tears. What could that joy have done for her, for him? Please, whoever you are, wherever you are, please, please let another's joy burn alight. #weNeedMoreLight

13. I am the sun. I am also the clouds; the storm, too.

14. I am the faded rainbow, where children dance in puddles, flouncing bonnets and skirts, rubber boots and bare foot splashes, in awe of all the muted colors.

15. These are the days. #donotforget

It's Sunday. Another day to love. Happy Sunday

Sunday Morning Ramblings: August 2017

1. Even in the midst of the storm there is always some form of a boat. Jump in. But you must paddle. #bebrave

2. Waiting for love takes time - like watching a clock and begging for that hour to pass - literally, taking your time. If you let go and live, instead of waiting, love will be present again, in the moment, if you are there, too. #belove

3. As many of you know, I've been married for a long time - to the same guy. His love for me never wavers. This love reminds me of that gorgeous painting *Lamia* by JW Waterhouse, or *La Belle Dame Sans Merci* by Sir Frank Dicksee; the maiden in her softness, heart on her sleeve, leaning against her soldier, regaled in his armor. #strengthandgentlenesstogether

4. On some days we are Leighton's *Accolade*, me conferring his knighthood. #mysoldier #hisqueen

5. On other days or in fleeting moments I am *The Tempest*. #theactualstorm

6. So how do any of us remain ourselves within this magical and daunting pairing? #haveNOclue

7. Marriage is an enigma. People are enigmas, too. #beyourself

8. Our daily actions/decisions require a higher purpose; one involving the whole/the unit/the family - ultimately the heart. If our hearts can beat as one...well, that's where love truly exists and surrenders.

9. I dreamed last night of a magic pen healing others.

10. In that same dream I was comforting Dean Martin, reminding him that while his youthful looks may be diminishing, if he took a moment and looked into his own eyes he'd find that young man again. #deanmartin?? #me??

11. Look into your eyes. #sheisthere #heisthere

12. My oldest is out driving with his dad right now. Life is so beautiful. He was just learning to walk a few hours ago. #time

13. I'm thinking of having an art sale on my front lawn. I've got so many paintings now. #maybeIcanletsomego #maybe

14. I am a lover. I truly do not know how to do this life any other way. #puresyrup #sapfromthetree

15. If love makes a way into your life, cherish it. If you are waiting for love, look in the mirror.

16. I love you.

It's Sunday Another day to love Happy Sunday

Love in its essence is spiritual fire.

Seneca

September

Sunday Morning Ramblings: September 2017

1. What is this insatiable need to be RIGHT?

2. Do many of us feel "WRONG" to begin with?

3. Constantly striving to always be "right" leaves us with a DISTANCING and nagging force posturing and proving someone or a group "wrong."

4. In today's society, disagreeing is no longer allowed. People are afraid.

5. If I disagree with you on something you feel/think is morally right, does that make me wrong?

6. What would happen if we just let it go and let God - whether it's God/the Universe/Spirit or simply our sanity and peace of mind - what would happen? Just leave it? LET IT BE? Stop policing everything?

7. Some would suggest that "letting it go" would create chaos? I disagree.

8. I've tried it. What I've witnessed happening is that as I no longer allow my inner chaos its reign, there is a prevailing current more powerful, within and without, affecting me and those around me. It's called PEACE. Its ripple effect is quite astonishing and awe inspiring.

9. Try it. Disengage. Or instead, speak the words to yourself that IT IS OKAY not to fight. Your inner fight shows up every second you engage in proving you're more right than someone else.

10. The anger/fight/contempt/arrogance is a VENEER. What's behind that? Certainly, not peace.

11. I'm a fighter. A warrior. But I'm also a peacemaker. A diplomat. And I am pretty much never afraid of confrontation. However, I PREFER PEACE to any of it.

12. Peace is where LOVE happens. Peace is where love expressed heals/comforts/repairs/restores/anchors...and the list goes on.

13. Why do we HIDE behind the veneer of rage? Ultimately, we NEVER WIN from that place.

14. "We will fight till the death." We shout and scream and kick and shove and push....and never, ever get to peace. Ever.

15. And to the death, we fight. And then we die. Was our death the reward?

It's Sunday. Another day to love. Happy Sunday

Sunday Morning Ramblings: September 2017

1. Did you realize you can grow while hanging off the cliff?

2. I was born hanging off a cliff.

3. Many of us are.

4. Did you know there could be growth even while we are clawing our way to the edge?

5. I didn't either...until I began to bloom.

6. My roots needed to find stability first.

7. Then the bloom can burst forth. The beginning is always a tiny seedling peaking out, among the harsh cliffs, jagged edges surrounding us. But hold on. Life is coming.

8. And when it does, that bloom, that shoot, that seedling, that giver of life, that living organism breathing oxygen into itself and those around us will reach for the sun; even, and especially, on the cloudiest, most dismal of days. Living and growing will take the place of everything else.

9. We may stand alone. We may be in the quiet, quite often. New growth can only be seen by those who wait.

10. Enduring patience.

11. When the moment comes to burst forth it is as though TIME never existed. It is as though TIME were nothing. Yet, it is only in time that we bloom.

12. Being afraid doesn't stop us.

13. Hanging on while letting go is the only choice.

14. The only choice. Oh, we may make other decisions, but in the shadow of our souls we remain clenched, begging for relief.

15. Our true choice remains like a sweet offering.

16. If we stay closed up, the reverberation will shake our core and those locked up with us. The outcome, death.

17. If we open ever-so-slightly, an abundant life rips the ground, tearing the Universe into celebratory confetti, bells chiming, thunderous applause. And this all while we're hanging on.

18. So. What are we waiting for?

It's Sunday. Another day to love. Happy Sunday.

The earth has music for those who listen.

Shakespeare

October

Sunday Morning Ramblings: October 2017

1. Men and women in power...tsk tsk. A true and natural leader never encourages fear from their platform. Best to walk away if we find ourselves in that space with them. #outthedoor

2. Then, whom do we walk towards? No one. All our power is within.

3. Outside voices never speak as coherent and peace-loving a language as the one we have inside of us.
#empowermentisNOTforthefearfulorweak
#theysimplyCANNOThearTHATvoice

4. Remember never to miss the quiet spaces in a conversation. Those moments may be the most precious and revealing. #listen

5. Hidden agendas somehow always make us feel exposed to something dangerous and uneasy...even if we don't understand what IT is. #walkaway #itisOK

6. Should there be levels of trust? Hmm. #ponderings

7. I'm making French toast while typing this.

8. If you had to give it ALL up to become WHO you truly are, would you?

9. What do we live for? And who? It changes like the seasons for me. Other than my guys always being the constant, do I remember to include my own heart in that snap shot called Life?

10. Speaking of seasons. Today, October won. #yesOctoberisaseason

It's Sunday. Another day to love. Happy Sunday.

Sunday Morning Ramblings: October 2017

1. If you were truly free, what would today look like for you? What would it feel like?

2. What is freedom? Is freedom enslavement to an ideal or a family or a people or a belief system? If you're in a box and the lid is open, are you able to climb out?

3. Sunday is a day; a perfect and splendid day, 24 hours to engage and laugh and love and enjoy and eat and smile and stretch and giggle and wonder and sleep and share and touch and taste and smell and notice and dream and walk and dance and bend and turn and live… just like all the other days.

4. Some souls are aching. I used to know them. I used to bring life to them. If their hands were reaching out to me I would gently take hold and remind them of who they truly are so they could begin to live again.

5. When we recognize our beauty, our heart, our truth, the desire for power is extinguished and its embers merely light our path instead.

6. I am a creator.

7. I love people.

8. Someone dear to me shoved me off a bridge the other day. But I always carry my net. So I didn't get harmed. And I still love her.

9. All this twisted mess about serving. Yuk. If you are told who to serve, you have a master. You are a slave. #nofreedom

10. Listen to your heart, pay attention to your soul, feel the wind on your face, slow down each day and who you are to love and be available to will be revealed like the gentle whisper of wisdom that it is. #trueservice

11. Mean people. Is that an oxymoron?

12. Something about the sea...

13. These are ramblings...

14. I've heard the truth eventually gets revealed. I'm beginning to think it's the lies that come into focus. #Isthatthesamething?

15. Gatherings are on my mind and in my heart. Lovely people, gorgeous food, blessed conversations...

16. Autumn is where it's at! #gettingourfallon

It's Sunday. Another day to love. Happy Sunday.

Sunday Morning Ramblings: October 2017

1. At the beginning of a climb I am extremely optimistic; enthusiasm breathing life into me. And then about three-quarters the way up, at times, I'm doubting my very existence as a human being. This is how it can be in life. Period.

2. If you are doubting, or fatigued, remember you could quite possibly be near the top with spectacular views. But it's always good to have a sit-down, a snack and a satisfying beverage anyway.

3. Me and my guy have a private joke between us. (no longer private after you read this) On our honeymoon, many moons

and many honeys ago, we were hiking in Colorado. A beautiful, grassy area with many smallish hills along the trail. The final destination atop a mountain with a lake plunked right down in its center or near its center. The map displayed the climb and the lake, but never told us how many hills we'd need to traverse before we got there. So along the way, up just about every hill, after the first 5 or so, EC would shout out, "This is it! Just over this hill is the lake!" We'd climb. No lake. After several of these shout outs we began fatigue-laughing. Up the hill we'd go. He'd shout out. We'd peer over. No lake. And on and on this went for miles. We did eventually get there.

4. So now, as we are climbing through life, we "shout out" to each other, "This is it! Just over this hill is the lake!"

5. Someone dear to me, in her rage, called me fake. As in not real. That is quite possibly the only thing I am not. Seriously, ask my mother. Ask my father. Ask my best friend. Ask anyone who truly knows and understands me. I realize her words were to appease a bad decision she had made. I wouldn't support her drama. Or her rage. And that decision couldn't get more real.

6. I spoke with some soldiers last night. I listened to them, too. My heart heard so much in those 4 hours. If you've never had the privilege to speak with a man or woman who has served or is serving I recommend it. You will see more clearly just how much is misunderstood about our world, our country.

7. Systems, governments, organizations, groups, studies are ALL FLAWED; every single one of them. Stop waiting for them to get their act together. Not a single one has accomplished that in the History of Forever.

8. The Honor Flight volunteer said something profound last night, "There are wonderful people in this world."

9. Good people just keep showing up. Be one of them.

10. I read something last night, on a friend's page. "Optimism is just another form of denial."

11. I'd like to say, "Optimism is a form of survival." In fact, optimism is survival. But we must be brave enough to acknowledge this and then share it. #donotbethestickinthemud

12. Stop giving your power to the group you abhor. Each time you "hate" on them, they've got you. However, hating on the group then means we don't need to be intimate. That is a real concern.

13. I trust people who have been in the trenches. #alloflifestrenches

14. We might be frolicking on a hay wagon today. Or at the very least, running wild in a pumpkin patch.

15. I love my friends.

16. I'm in such a place right now....such a place. But hold fast.
This is it. Just over this hill, is the lake!

It's Sunday. Another day to love. Happy Sunday.

Friendship is always a sweet responsibility never an opportunity.

Kahlil Gibran

Sunday Morning Ramblings: November 2017

1. Going through fire will harm us. Going through fire will change us, mold us. Going through fire will refine us. Going through fire will, in its graciousness, warm us to such a degree that we may burn with life and living.

2. Creating love is an art form. Love may be void or hidden deep inside, needing to be chiseled out; the sculptor's hands being sensitive to Love's whereabouts. Love may be closer to the surface, yet, most times buried deep inside a dense stone. With skill, the sweeping movement of a rasp, pieces begin their descent to the ground. The process, at times challenging even the most experienced artist, takes time. However, creating love that's been hidden always takes the perfect amount of time. There is never a wait, only a tender longing.

3. I call on the angels for assistance.

4. I thoroughly enjoyed waking up at...7, 6, 8, oh, whatever time it was. edited: I thoroughly enjoyed waking up. #fallisfall #timeistime #savingtime?

5. Parents: When your teenager meets the challenge stating this will define how he proceeds as a success or failure in life.

Me: Being mentored by my son.
#bebrave #theyareOURteachers #parentsdonotalwaysRULE

6. The outcome may not always be the reward. Perhaps simply doing IT (whatever it is) has always been the reward. #growth #learning

7. We can play this game of life on a higher plane - in any moment, at any given time. We simply choose. #choosehighly

8. I love a lot of the words of spiritual teachings. I'm reading everything again. It's who I am. It's who I ever was, forever. I'm so happy to be back with myself. #reunion

9. The church, the synagogue, the field, the mosque, the shrine, the temple, they are real only if they exist in your heart. If they do not, keep searching. hint: look within #notforthefaint #notfortheweak #notfortheEGO

10. My prayer is not heard more clearly where the stained glass hangs. My prayer is heard. Period. #listen

11. My circle was broken several years ago. Recently, I have come 'round full again, to the lovely beginning. We get to do that. And it's so much more beautiful this time. #thankful

12. Pain is lessened when we let go.

13. Hate can only exist if we dwell in our mind, alone -the pathway to the heart cut off. The head never has all clarity. The valve must be open. Free to think. Free to feel.

14. When we get to love, all is well, forever.

15. Weeping is sometimes the only way for me to get to my joy.

It's Sunday. Another day to love. Happy Sunday.

Sunday Morning Ramblings: November 2017

1. At times, my sadness envelops me like a warm covering, protection from the noise, where I burrow inside a sweet dwelling place that offers great wisdom.

2. Sadness, heartache, loss, injury can be our greatest strengths where new dimensions and deeper love may be restored and returned to ourselves.

3. If we are rich, is there truly a reason to get richer?

4. If we are content, should our days be spent seeking more contentment?

5. Lemon water makes life better.

6. Are we on the waters of life in a ship of fools?

7. There are TAKERS and there are GIVERS in our lives. When I couldn't find my footing, fear and doubt had me grabbing at life in desperation. When I realized that my feet were never dangling, life came to me, sat with me, was my teacher.

8. If you are a teacher, you MUST be a student, ALWAYS. Otherwise, your students will truly NEVER learn a single thing - and they will exist with desperation, feet dangling from on top of cliffs.

9. I feel the Universe's hand today.

10. Stop. Just let yourself stop. If it's too much trouble for yourself, do it for the people who love you.

11. Our 17yo scored 19 points in his BB scrimmage game the other night. He was so humble about it. Did he get that from me? LOL

12. I love to laugh. If you know me, you know I love to laugh.

13. Two different people have called my telephone after they died - both while I lived in NYC. One, I spoke with, the other left a message with my roommate while I sat and listened. Both experiences were life affirming. And proof that the spirit LOVES LIFE and LIVING.

14. Being transparent is the only way to the truth. FOREVER. It's the only way to PEACE. FOREVER. It's the only way to WISDOM, HEALING, METAMORPHOSIS. Find the people you can be real with. It will help you along. But more importantly, BE TRANSPARENT with YOUR SELF. Your soul will mend a thousand tragic and empty lifetimes.

15. Even while wounded, we begin to heal.

16. If you don't like where you are, then move. You are not a tree. But if you like where you are, don't forget to grow like one.

It's Sunday. Another day to love. Happy Sunday.

Sunday Morning Ramblings: November 2017

1. I believe in a love so strong.

2. I have witnessed a love so strong.

3. I am the recipient of a love so strong.

4. I am the giver of a love so strong.

5. I didn't always know strong love, as a giver or receiver.

6. Loving strong is void of the self, the ego, the complainer, the victim and the victor. It is for everyone in the room, in the present; it is the true gift.

7. Loving strong makes no demands, claims no prizes, wins no awards.

8. Strong love is brave. It's waiting and hoping, enduring.

9. Strong love is only ever in the moment; strung together like rare pearls, dangling beauty; simply.

10. Loving so strong keeps broken hearts beating, weak minds lifted and shattered souls burning with life.

11. Strong love received and given must be let go.

12. Strong love is not a possessor. We never own it. Strong love is only ever cherished, acknowledged, embraced, then, always released.

13. If not released, then we are murderers, torturers, vagrants, impoverished, abusers, crooks, swindlers, liars, empty - doing time in our own self-made prison.

14. Loving so strong is the gatekeeper - handling the keys, breaking loose the shackles, stumbling from the gallows, our hood removed, the sun's rays aflame on our soul after the

longest, harshest, dim lit and blackest days of a life we have never fully lived we are then made free...

15. ...with a love so strong.

It's Sunday. Another day to love. Happy Sunday

One word frees us of all the weight and pain of life; that word is love.

Sophocles

December

Sunday Morning Ramblings: December 2017
*warning: heart on sleeve, read at your own risk

1. This whole idea of "me being here" doesn't really feel like LIFE unless I'm living. You too?

2. Can we heal the past? What if someone, or many someones have harmed us, emotionally? Can we go back to that time and space and heal it all? Chime in, if you know.

3. I was reading the news this morning, which I haven't done and won't continue to do on a regular basis and realized just how these voices can make you believe anything with a simple headline. #makingstupidpeoplein5wordsorless

4. Headlines. Is that what your life is about? Or are you the context of the story, living out and appreciating the details, fact checking your own decisions, quandaries, reactions? If we only live life as a headline or worse, make someone else a headline, we've missed the entire story...forever...making our experience with them nothing more valid or useful than kindling for the fire, and worse. We stand by and watch it burn.

5. Truly listening is the only way to know the story. And if we can listen with our hearts, instead of our minds, then our

relationships flourish. If we don't listen this way, then our hearts break. Our hearts are in our bodies, not only to beat, but to keep us alive...with others.

6. My closest relationships with friends and family members have changed dramatically over the last 6 months. There is a shift. And while I can process and understand shifts very well...and accept them, I am at a loss, feeling the loss...still.

7. Is there anything we can do about loss? Do we fill the space it once occupied? Do we have the right to? Is there room? Or was that, which was in that space, crowding out inspiration and movement?

8. Forfeiting inspiration is against my inner religion/belief system/heart. I can no longer do it. Inspiration is sustenance.

9. I'd like to blame someone for all the lies. There is a liar in our midst. And yet, blame is a severe, unrelenting road block.

10. I am heartbroken.

11. I am also brave.

12. Recently, I was left out of a family member's upcoming wedding. This broke me. It still breaks me, especially since I've loved her so very much her entire life. Yet, all my psycho-analytical study concludes it's more about her than me. So why

do I feel so horrible still? And was that her plan? Gosh this stuff is so awful. #hurtingpeoplehurtspeople #honestyisleftoutofmanytodos

13. New relationships are beginning in my life. New avenues to explore. New histories to listen to and more love for the being who shares them with me. #truerelationships

14. The words I type are me. They always have been and they always will be. I am my words. I am my word. If they are misinterpreted it has nothing to do with me. Perhaps the heart is reading them incorrectly, if at all. I am also my deeds. Those who have seen me in action know what I'm talking about. #giver

15. If this was heavy, I make no apologies. Saying I'm sorry only comes when I've harmed someone or made a mistake. I will never apologize for feeling or being me.

16. Thank God I have the memory of those black sneakers when I was a pre-teen. My mother searched high and low for them. I never wanted to be like everyone else. Fitting in was defined by my own skin, not someone else's. And now, in my 50s, I am defining my skin again. #freedom #theunknown

17. When we love, we may lose, but not because of love. Love is a force - opening doors, creating oxygen where there was none. Love is delicate, too, unassuming. Love is courageous, stepping into the unknown, diving off the cliffs. It is a transparency that

only the starved, undernourished crave and long for, when we've finally had enough of a void so deep and dark and lonely. Love comes in to rescue us. Love shows up continuously, whether we are aware or not. It is there. And will remain. And never leave.

18. I am so very sad today. I am also, so very grateful. I have 3 very dedicated and wonderful men in my life who love me unconditionally, unwavering. Three men who show me that ALL that I do, ALL that I say means something, so very wonderful and special to them. I thank God for them.

It's Sunday Another day to love. Happy Sunday

Sunday Morning Ramblings: December 2017

1. It IS Sunday, right?

2. Sending cards out after the holidays is totally acceptable. I've never refused one. #takingthefamilyphotomighthappen

3. So here we are again. The holidays. Or Holy Days. Or Whole Days. Or simply days. But probably, just dazed.

4. To stay centered and focused during this time of the year, I purposely leave everything until the last minute. #baking #cooking #wrapping #screaming
5. I've been using Frankincense all year.

6. I follow the stars all year, as well.

7. I don't identify as a Christian. I never have. Seriously, when I was a kid I used to tell everyone I was a "person."

8. Back then, (I say "back then" now) no one seemed too crazy about identity or so it seemed.. If you were a decent human being that's all that mattered. Thankful for my parents and grandmother for that thinking! Gram was Eastern Orthodox with a dash of mysticism and Transcendentalism and...I loved her. My dad ripped us out of catechism when we were little. The priest was an ogre. Then we moved onto...something else for another 5 minutes. I'm glad I wasn't raised with religion. It can lock people up too tightly. I like to be free. I think God works best with freedom. They're friends. Freedom and God. Good buddies, actually.

9. While I lived in NYC I dated a Jewish man. His religion centered me. I related to the words in the Torah. It gave me a grounding I had never had because of the traditions and the family wisdom. I soaked it in. I fell in love with his entire family. And they fell in love with me. It was a miraculous time. I was young.

10. Those young moments can alter us on deep levels.

11. Then I met a man who, when he was younger, married a Jewish woman. He's the most solid, grounded person I've ever

known. He grew up with his first wife's family. He received from them exactly what I received from my NYC experience and then some. We are now married to each other. #EC

12. We observe both Jewish and Christian as well as Transcendental traditions and values in our home. It's so lovely. And so free.

13. We are all thinkers here. We are all artists. We are all lovers. We are all poets. We love the spirit of truth, whether from a song, a word, a book, nature, our soul or someone else's or simply dropped down from the sky.

14. We are not afraid of truth. Ultimately, it is all that Love ever could be.

15. Dad, you are missing so much. Your grandsons are the spirit of who you yearn to be. They are the perfect gift for you. My husband, the perfect friend. Your choices keep you away from a love so strong...

16. Our traditions strengthen us. Our beliefs give us something to hope for. But alas, we are human beings with broken hearts, sad times, uncomfortable experiences who still... STILL have the desire for LOVE in the midst of every season of our lives.

17. Wherever you are right now as you read this, I hope your spirit feels love whatever you're celebrating. Because even a little

love is still Love. And it is enough to hold onto and get to the next moment...where love can happen again.

It's Sunday. Another day to love. Happy Sunday.

Sunday Morning Ramblings: 2017 approaching 2018

1. A love letter to 2017.

2. Dear Year, you've been so good to us. A full, and overflowing 36almost5 days of abundant love.

3. Everyday, even in a small way, which can NEVER EVER be small, really, Love showed up.

4. At times, Love arrived on our front porch either in a box or dish, wrapped with a sweet smile, warm hands. Other times, 2017, you made a way for us to love others in our home, with our prayers or in a song.

5. Dear Year, your days, sometimes windy, rainy and stormy allowed calm to pass through our souls, even as the windows rattled and our trees lost their limbs.

6. We've had to sever some long standing branches, making way for new growth. This is simply how some years are.

7. 2017, your lessons were many, offering us choices, strengthening us whole.

8. Even in our tears, you were there with another day, another chance to alter the wrongs, offer the forgiveness, waking us with a bright sun.

9. You are a gift loaded with hours, for us. Minutes to stand by. Moments to capture.

10. The morning broke 365 times, for each of us, individually and collectively. And every night sky creating a path, that even in our dreams, is leading us on to gorgeous, hopeful views even if we lay our heads in despair, hope is made new when we, once again, open our eyes at dawn.

11. We make plans, organize cupboards and drawers, while you linger, gently approaching the next minute, hour.

12. If it weren't for you, Dear Year, I wouldn't be here...in this exacting period in time, where possibilities can be claimed, and dreams realized, warm embraces shared.

13. Another day, another day, another day, another day to deliver, to become, to offer, to hold, to remember. Another day...to love.

14. 2017, we value you, your richness in each 24 hour, 1,440 minute day. Days that weave together rich hues of the year's tapestry.

15. Each year we can create more beauty and luster, more willingness, more deep, complete breaths.

16. Dear Year, you've brought new friends, which at this time in life, is bold. We are forever grateful.

17. And while this year, this 2017, may appear to have an end, it is only the turning of the page - the book, still being written.

18. Thank you, Dear Year, for all of it.

It's Sunday. Another day to love. Happy Sunday.

2018

Do not go where the path may lead, go instead where there is no path and create a trail.

Ralph Waldo Emerson

January

Sunday Morning Ramblings: January 2018

1. When something moves us, we can receive this piece of art into our beings. We can allow ourselves to be forever changed. Our cells revived. Our spirits renewed. Our canvas colored. Art is everywhere and in everything. It is all that we are.

2. Love and Art are pals, the sort who hold hands, even in public.

3. If every emotion were a door, would you walk through to find yourself, perhaps more complete on the other side?

4. Feelings are inside of us for a serious, deep, victorious reason.

5. Understanding what we feel can be a challenge. Feeling those feelings can be even more difficult. Do it anyway.

6. If we keep running from something, we will eventually circle around and meet up with it again.

7. So within this whimsical existence, can we be brave enough to meet our fears head on? Confront them? Hand on our sword, at the ready?

8. I'm longing to lie on a bed of greens.

9. Ramblings, remember?

10. So while our lives here up north are covered with white fluff and crust, I will EAT a bed of greens instead.

11. Greens make us braver.

12. Greens are our sword.

13. Greens keep us safe, too.

14. Greens are wild and full of life.

15. However, it isn't easy being green. But it sure can mean everything, whether we lie on them or eat them. #Greens #Wild and #FullofLife

It's Sunday. Another day to love. Happy Sunday

Sunday Morning Ramblings: January 2018

1. Love is hard for some folks. Really hard. Having high expectations that others should love them first, without any such love flowing back, demanding they are deserving of love with an

arrogant stance can only lead me to believe one ONE thing about that person or people...they do not love themselves.

2. When we love ourselves, we have the capacity to love others.

3. How do we love ourselves? We get to know who we are. All the bits, the broken and shattered pieces, the bent angles with singed edges, the crumbles...pick them up...gather them together. And then love that mosaic. Because you survived.

4. Our survival was the direct result of love. There can be no other way. That force alone can save a life, any life, from the mountaintop to the valley and on into the cave.

5. The form love takes on, most times, is in muted tones as a backdrop, showing up unexpectedly, but with the life-affirming effect to steady us, hold us, keep us from falling.

6. If we happen to fall, love shows up. And keeps showing up, ad infinitum.

7. What else could it be then, if not love? If science or biology or intellect are our answers to this question, read #5. See?

8. It's been love all along. Every person, every word, every challenge, every instance, in every storm, love has been at the ready.

9. Why do I write and speak of such a seemingly common enigma, one whose Oxford definition barely scratches the surface?

10. It is who I am. I will never be able to be anything else. You either?

11. I told my Grandmother when I was a child I would wait WAIT forever for love. She smiled. Love was standing right next to me, a backdrop in muted tones wearing an apron.

12. So on this journey of life and living, what is it that seizes our beings, captures our hearts, encompasses our minds, even in the void we wait for it, even just a trickle of it, arms stretched out, more than any feeling, thought, plan, change, happening, celebration, or word?

13. Love.

14. It's the answer. In the tunnel. In the blackness. In the fire. In the storm. In the chamber. In the prison. In the solitude. In the wind. In our loneliness. In our pain.

15. And...in our joy.

16. Who are you? Get to know yourself. Don't be too afraid. In case you are, love will take care of that.

It's Sunday. Another day to love. Happy Sunday.

Sunday Morning Ramblings: January 2018

1. Let your soul be your guide.

2. What song speaks to your heart?

3. Sing that one.

4. Our bodies do have something to do with our realities. Of course, our brains for all that thinking/planning/dealing, and our muscle and sinew for getting to and fro, and our organs for the seemingly endless effort of keeping us all alive and going, hopefully, and with much assistance from ourselves, healthfully BUT but BuT what of our soul, our spirit, our power? What makes that go? What kills it? What brings it back to life after it's been dead for eons or a week or years?

5. If you have an inkling of what gives it life, do that - even for a moment. Do it. Whatever it is that makes you live again, whatever makes you love again, whatever makes you YOU again, please do that. Please. I beg. Yes, I'm begging. The more souls who are alive, the more souls who come back from the dead, the more ALIVE and WELL we ALL can become. The more alive and well we become, the greater the ripple effect is to

move those mountains and build those dreams and create that soul-satisfying life we all ALL crave.

6. What are you craving?

7. Our cravings are varied. Don't be shy about yours, especially to yourself, even if only to yourself. Do not hide from yourself, your TRUE self.

8. Of course, it is perfectly OK to make it a private matter. However, the power POWER is so great that even if it is tucked inside a secret pocket, behind a closed door, locked in a special box, it will have an EFFECT on those around you because others will sense that power Power POWER - that beautiful soul power. SOUL POWER engages life. Soul power does not hide, because it CANNOT hide itself.

9. It is brighter than the sun.

10. BRIGHTER THAN THE SUN!

11. Naysayers, you say? Naysayers are only capable of saying, "nay." Just keep movin' along.

12. We canNOT do anything for those beings, except BE the POWER, the SOUL -on fire- POWER. Those negative voices will either burn or...they will BURN.

13. ...burn back to life!

14. This is how we stay alive. But we must MUST live, truly live, in order to BE ALIVE.

It's Sunday Another day to love Happy Sunday

Sunday Morning Ramblings: January 2018

1. Is it harsh enough that the world around us is constantly trying to break us, harm us? Then we learn that someone in our personal world is trying to do the same thing. What must we do?

2. I'm teaching my sons to stand up to it.

3. I'm learning to stand up to it.

4. My guy has stood up to it since the peace marches in the 60s, and no doubt before that time.

5. Love is power. Standing up against hurtful people and their malcontent, whether they think it's so or not, means nada, is what must be done. Unafraid. If we were to create the story, remove the names, they'd think it was hurtful too. (We all have to be made aware of our actions/words/behavior. None of us are exempt.)

6. The dawning comes only ONLY when the light is shining. Be the light.

7. Repeating what the group, any group, says is not and NEVER will be our personal voice. It will merely be a louder version of the group's voice. I never NEVER want the group to speak for me. If you believe God/Universe created you, individually, why would you believe HIS/HER/God's voice is to be heard collectively? Seems counter-intuitive, that one, going against free will and even, infringing on the idea that we are made as individuals, not as groups. Group voices keep us separated, alone, lonely. The group also is where the weak stand, separated, alone, lonely.

8. Finding our voices...oh boy...is certainly not easy. But once we do...my hope is that the echo extends itself like a branch capturing the fledgling falling from its nest; my hope is that the echo is carried on a small seed, planting itself in the heart of someone whose world around them is trying to crush and silence their true voice; my hope is that the echo whispers into the soul of another reminding them of their value/their worth/their hope/their dreams.

9. What is our TRUE VOICE? In some of us, it lays dormant, breathing deeply, waiting for the perfect moment to speak. In others, that voice is our heartbeat, our song, our palette, our poetry. And in others, our true voice is the one we hear speak to us through another who has found his/her voice, speaking it

aloud and as it dances through the airwaves our heart is captivated and moved by its perfection; thus opening a beautiful space for our own voice to be spoken.

10. A sweet friend of mine wrote the other day that she wanted to believe there was good left in the world.

11. Thoughts?

12. Everyone here knows what I believe. However, the true answer is in our own heart. If we can open our hearts to love, even a teeny speck of it, we will begin to, not only believe, but actually see how much good is, not only left, but in abundance and overflowing.

13. And when we see this THIS truth, our voices will dust themselves off, cough a bit, perhaps shake, and begin to speak unafraid, with great power and spirit. Those whose souls need to hear will be waiting with relief.

14. My coffee mug is almost empty. I've got textbook chapters to read and a paper to write. #counselor

15. I'm beginning to find my voice.

It's Sunday. Another day to love. Happy Sunday.

Be not afraid of growing slowly, be afraid only of standing still.

Chinese Proverb

February

1. Let's talk about our children. Why are THEY here?

2. Would our answer be the same answer we'd give to ourselves and why we are here? It should be, right?

3. As parents, our training and rearing and loving and supporting should go as far as it can and then....deep breath here...no really, all of us, EXHALE and then...we need to LET THEM GO.

4. They are not extensions of ourSELVES. They are not here to prove to the world, especially *that awful one* that broke us, that we are whole WHOLE or holy. They are not here to live out our fantasies, our dreams, our desires. That would actually be going against God/Universe. Why? Because, then we put ourselves in the position as all powerful, all knowing. Oz. Truth is, we are masquerading/hiding behind a curtain if we think so. Let's face this ALL together, Mom/Dad, we are NOT all knowing. And that, IS, honestly, OK. Besides, our children already know this about us. They wish we'd let them BE who they are, or at least allow a little space on the path for them to navigate THEIR OWN JOURNEY.

5. Parenting is hard. However, living our lives authentically is EVEN harder. Yes. It's true. Examining our motives, owning our garbage, our egos, our failures, admitting our mistakes/shortcomings, accepting our limitations is EXACTLY why FAITH, TRUST, BELIEFS are available to us at every twist, turn, and broken bridge.

6. Constantly trying to make our children BE this or BE that not only breaks their hearts and spirits, it SHATTERS OURS.

7. Anger is the sign. Look for the sign. It's there. Our anger. Or theirs. Another sign is the aura of "failure" they may be wearing. Look for those signs.

8. Do our children come here to stroke our egos, make us look better, become little dangling bits off of our beings OR are they here to cling for a time and then BE, live out their lives, the way they NEED to for their soul's purpose?

9. Imagine interfering in someone's soul purpose. Somebody point me to the confessional booth, call the rabbi, book me a trip to India! Quick!

10. Our hope is that our children LOVE us, LIKE us, TRUST us. If we show them the possibility of LOVE and TRUST, by allowing them to GROW at their own pace, without our disastrous egos, they'll fly! And they will LOVE us for it. And they will TRUST us forever.

11. If we never show them the FAITH we have in the process, not the faith we have in them, but the faith we have in life and living, authentically, they will MOST definitely grow to become replicas of ourSELVES - but NOT the good bits, THE SHATTERED BITS. In some circles, it's referred to as "the sins of the father."

12. Parents have a tough job. Seriously, tough. But what makes it even harder, day in and day out, is when we neglect that FAITH (not religion) plays an enormous role here.

13. I'm not talking about religion or going to church or synagogue, temple or any other meeting place. This is deeper. This is true FAITH. Anyone can show up to a building for an hour or two. It's what's INSIDE YOUR SOUL when you pull out of the parking lot. See? Much deeper.

14. Years ago, when I was a brand new mother; only 5 years in, our son was taking violin lessons. Each day I would set him up to practice. PRACTICE PRACTICE PRACTICE. Oy. It was the most forced, uncomfortable experience of our lives together. I still apologize to him. He hated it; as in HATED every second of it. But feeling the inner pressure to have him succeed burned inside me. *failure alert! The torch was white hot in my soul to get this boy to play the violin. WTH?! When that didn't work, because thank HEAVENS, he was brave enough to tell me he HATED it (I was trapped in some delusional burning blaze in my being and couldn't see a thing other than that godforsaken violin), we moved onto the cello. Honestly, you can't make this

stuff up. lol *painful Well, you guessed it, oh wise people, he HATED the cello, too. Needless to say, we left the music school. This THIS is how I know there is a GOD. lol The relief was immediate. My SOUL, true nature, welcomed me home with OPEN ARMS. My son was so HAPPY - HAPPY LIKE FOR THE REST OF HIS LIFE - HAPPY! I have never NEVER forced anything on him since then. (he's not into social media so he can't argue with me here) But friends, you get the point, right?

15. His SOUL said NO WAY. He was in my care. He was little enough to stay in my house. And thankfully I WOKE UP. It reminded me of how my BEAUTIFUL SOUL was always getting crushed when I was a child by being FORCED to perform in some fashion.

16. We must get to the place where we FORGIVE OURSELVES. We've all made these errors as parents. We aren't PERFECT after all. However, the perfection is actually available to us when we are HONEST and AUTHENTIC with our children. The GREATEST TEACHER is being REAL. The GREATEST TEACHER is being TRUTHFUL about our failings. But nothing compares to the WIND OF FREEDOM our children inhale and fly with, than the parent who is BRAVE ENOUGH to allow their son/daughter space for their OWN SOUL to take FLIGHT.

17. Moms and Dads, I'm cheering us on from the stands!

It's Sunday. Another day to love. Happy Sunday.

Sunday Morning Ramblings: February 2018

1. 11:45am and the ramblings are a comin'.

2. When poetry isn't enough to fix your life...wait. Poetry is the ONLY thing that can fix a life.

3. EC and I were reflecting the other day on how many liars there are in the world. Right under our noses. Standing at podiums. Misinterpreting this and that. Making people feel so awful, deeply awful and afraid.

4. What is more astonishing is that there are more people following these liars than there are liars.

5. Conclusion: People are definitely afraid of the truth.

6. ...especially afraid of their own heart and soul truth. They have been taught NOT to trust their own soul...via the middle man. #profiteers

7. Truth is scary. I get it.

8. How long does a person stay in a place of lies following the arrogance of the groupthink? Years? Lifetimes?

9. When the soul begins to speak, look out. It's gonna be a day. #whoa

10. Enough about that.

11. I'm writing a paper today for my clinic class. I'm also going hiking with my guys. Then I'm going to take a nap. Not sure about the order of these events.

12. What if there was no religion? What if people weren't made to believe in something only outside themselves? #duality

13. I suppose we'll never know the answer to that one. And it's a biggie. Rats. Didn't I say, enough about that?

14. I have so many questions. Very few answers.

15. Pretty sure poetry can fix a life though.

It's Sunday. Another day to love. Happy Sunday.

Don't only practice your art, but force your way into its secrets; art deserves that for it and knowledge can raise man to the divine.

Ludwig von Beethoven

march

Sunday Morning Ramblings: March 2018

1. Let's simply be in awe of one another. Not proud. Just awe! #NoOneElseLikeYou #NoOneElseLikeMe

2. True care, for another, is a gift. It's also a power; a power to adjust whatever is wrong and mend it, make it right.

3. Bullying by coaches, teachers, pastors, preachers, parents is NOT and NEVER will be love. Actions speak the loudest. However, a big voice can make a soul crumble into tiny bits. Usually behind that big voice is a bully - weak man or woman parading around to get attention at all costs – usually at the expense of the lives of those who love them and, at the cost of their own life, as well.

4. Arrogance sucks! It literally sucks the life out of relationships, businesses, events, gatherings, all of life. The arrogant man or woman begins to wear it, looking drained of their life force, their love force. Shriveled skin, squinty puffy eyes, always busy and self-important.

5. I weep for the children of bullies. I weep for my own sons at the hands of the bully.

6. The law is written on our hearts. If our law is love and truth, we have no need to prove anything. #justbe

7. It's sunny today. I'm glad because the weariness of humanity's errors and ego can keep a heart weighted down. #goingforahiketoday

8. Yet, in any moment, we can get back to love and feel LIGHTer again.

9. I'm not there just yet. Forgive me, friends. I feel so deeply.

10. Teaching our sons the value of being authentic and honest rocks the boats of this world. This world is so full of traps and lies, men and women walking around acting as if they know something important.

11. It is the heart that knows. Not the mind.

12. Soul care is a precious and noble undertaking. I've been asked to be its facilitator. I am in awe. #onlyOneMe #onlyOneYou

13. Take care of your soul today. Do something authentic, honest. Don't allow another moment to go by without acknowledging the beauty and wisdom of what makes YOU so wonderful, unique and perfect.

14. Everyone in your world needs the TRUE YOU. It's what keeps hope and love alive. Thank you.

It's Sunday. Another day to love. Happy Sunday

Sunday Morning Ramblings: March 2018

1. ...because the clocks in our house read: 11:03am

2. I've been thinking about love. I know you're surprised. But seriously. Do you ever just sit and think about it?

3. I love LOVE, with all my heart, soul, mind, spirit.

4. Whenever I think about Love, a warm feeling rushes through me, as if my veins had fallen asleep at other times without it. Or have existed in a state of drudgery, pushing and pulling my blood through each vessel, barely making it. Then Love happens. My veins come alive, stretching this way and that. My brain is activated; memories of my true purpose, my true existence, my true meaning, and placement here on the planet awakened. #thoughts

5. So what then does the act of love do for us? #miracles

6. There was a college fund ad some years ago (almost 50) that stated, "A mind is a terrible thing to waste." I'd like to see an ad

that states, "A heart is a terrible thing to waste." Or, "A soul is a terrible thing to waste." Or "A spirit is a terrible thing to waste."

7. Our minds work overtime. Every minute, every second of every hour it is our minds that are never wasting anything except perhaps what our hearts, souls, and spirits are trying to say. #cantheygetawordin

8. This is precisely why I have chosen (or it has chosen me) to become a counselor. #soul #spirit

9. There is more to life than what meets the eye.

10. If we have a job to do, it's best to get on it!

11. Mother and son will be graduating around the same time. Surreal. If someone had told me this would be happening...well, honestly, I think I would have been thrilled, while at the same time wondering how I'd get here.

12. And if someone had told me what I'd need to go through to get here, I would have put on my running shoes!! #noway

13. Our life lessons can be put to good use, with our hearts open.

14. Thanks for hanging with me on this wild journey. I truly mean that. My heart and soul thank you.

15. I hope you continue to be a part of this collective ride. We are in this together, after all. #love #kindreds

16. Be where the light is. If you can't find it. Turn yourself on!

It's Sunday. Another day to love. Happy Sunday

Know how to listen, and you will profit even from those who talk badly.

Plutarch

April

Sunday Morning Ramblings: April 2018

1. We rose today. It was an absolute miracle; a for real miracle. #fevers #coughs #stuffyheads #crying #congestion #shakysleep #morecrying

2. When things need NEED to get done and our life is on hold, is our life on hold? Or is this, simply, our life?

3. Today is Passover: the major Jewish spring festival that commemorates the liberation of the Israelites from Egyptian slavery, lasting seven or eight days from the 15th day of Nisan. Origin from pass over 'pass without touching,' with reference to the exemption of the Israelites from the death of their firstborn (Exod. 12).

4. Today is Easter: the most important and oldest festival of the Christian Church, celebrating the resurrection of Jesus Christ and held (in the Western Church) between March 21 and April 25, on the first Sunday after the first full moon following the northern spring equinox. The period in which Easter occurs, especially the weekend from Good Friday to Easter Monday. Origin Old English ēastre ; of Germanic origin and related to German Ostern and east. According to Bede the word is derived from Ēastre, the name of a goddess associated with spring.

5. Today is also April Fools: an annual celebration in some European and Western countries commemorated on April 1 by playing practical jokes and spreading hoaxes. The jokes and their victims are called April fools. People playing April Fool jokes often expose their prank by shouting "April fool" at the unfortunate victim(s).

6. All 3 of the above mentioned holidays can NOT be proven by historians to be historically accurate or even pieced together to be based on real facts with accurate sources. Grand assumptions were made to create holidays which have become money-making schemes for churches, synagogues, Hallmark, candy makers, etc.

7. I was shocked to discover this! Not the money-making part...all the other bits.

8. What does this reveal about us as people? I believe the answer is multi-layered.

9. First, most of the world's population NEEDS to believe in something BIGGER and GRANDER than itself.

10. Second, we MUST and NEED to see/feel/believe that we CAN OVERCOME and RISE AGAIN.

11. Third, apparently, most of humanity DESIRES a reason to be with one another that is HIGHER in meaning than simply...being together. And, like we really need a reason to eat chocolate. Ha!

12. Fourth, I abhor practical jokes. However, I LOVE to LAUGH...so my guess is that LAUGHTER is required for most of us to be free from our troubles, free from our worries, thus LIFTING US HIGHER...which brings us right back around to the crucifixion and rising, brings us around to being freed from some form of slavery.

13. Promises kept are truly lovely. Believing in something more profound than our flesh is rejuvenating and full of hope.

14. But I'm beginning to wonder when humanity decided that playing pranks was a good thing. Hmm.
#whoisthejokeonanyway

15. Whatever we believe or don't believe, whatever we hold onto and value or don't hold onto and don't value my HOPE is that we RISE and are FREE.

16. Because that is a STATE of the HEART and there is NO historian who could ever PROVE or DISPROVE what DWELLS deep within each one of us.

It's Sunday. Another day to love. Happy Sunday

Sunday Morning Ramblings: April 2018

1. Love remains the most powerful force in all the land.

2. Practice loving people right where they are - and wait for the gift you'll receive. Your own heart will show up and present itself.

3. When we give to others we are the gift. So are they.

4. Loneliness is the avoidance of our own self love. That is part of the reason we can sit in a group of people and feel alone.

5. So how do we learn to love ourselves?

6. Love each other.

7. How do we love each other? Read #2.

8. I've begun a new ritual. When I wake up each day I simply whisper, "Thank you." #afteraNaptoo

9. Do not fear authenticity. It is the closest thing to God / Truth we can be on this earth.

10. It's not all deep thoughts today. I'm also wondering what to make for dinner right now.

11. This year, in upstate New York, we are living through a period known as The 6-month Winter.

12. If you're wondering what to do today, do something you've never done before. Jump out of the box of life and live a little differently. See what happens to your spirit.

13. I've heard that spirits love to soar!

It's Sunday Another day to love. Happy Sunday

Sunday Morning Ramblings: April 2018

1. The apparition of doubt: let's speak directly to this.

2. It stands next to us, all of us, whispering, perhaps shouting, "You can't do this!" "You can't do that!"

3. At times its voice ends with an exclamation point! Other times, it's a breathy whisper ending with an emphatic period. In moments of inspiration, it shows up, voices its demands and leaves with a trail of dots... That's what I call "leaving its mud-sodden footprints all over the place." Such a mess!

4. Change is demanding. Change is tiring. Change is sometimes very sad. Change causes separation. In those moments the apparition of doubt seems tall, large, loud, foreboding.

5. But I've learned that it is simply a voice waiting to be addressed. Tell it what you think.

6. If you don't agree or believe it, say it.

7. "Not today!" "Not now!" "You don't get to speak here."

8. As inspiration joyfully approaches, the apparition of doubt steps in.

9. He/She/It has had the front row and center stage for a l-o-n-g time.

10. As creation and inspiration, ideas full of life, begin to flood in, the voice of doubt may get louder.

11. But like the roaring lion devouring who it MAY, let it run past you. Let its roar become a piece of the music. Let its fierce energy transport you to your destination.

12. Power is only power where we allow it. The apparition of doubt has no real power. It's a ghost.

13. Perhaps a ghost of the past, or the present or the future. Wherever your fear sits and waits, is where it will dwell.

14. Give it some attention but do tell it to go.

15. This life, the one you've been given, is for the voice of the living. The voice of the ghost is dead.

16. Where there is life there is power! True power exists where creativity and inspiration are honored and allowed to speak.

17. Your voice needs to be heard. My prayer is that we all get to "speak" - our inspiration, our art, our words, our hearts, our souls.

18. Without YOU the world loses some of its life and breath - making the rest of us gasp for air. YOU are someone's oxygen. Remember to breathe! Give life by living FULLY with the inhalation of inspiration and the exhalation of creation and observe your LIFE and those around you in FULL BLOOM!

It's Sunday Another day to love Happy Sunday

I don't think of all the misery but of the beauty that still remains.

Anne Frank

may

Sunday Morning Ramblings: May 2018

1. I've been CRYING since last night. Cried myself to sleep.
Woke up this morning, TEARS cascading...

2. This is how it is when one's soul witnesses a HEART breaking
OPEN.

3. On this side of a heart BREAK, we imagine being overcome by
the dark. What if, we are OVERCOME by the LIGHT?

4. What if our HEART, once opened, becomes a gateway to our
TRUE self, our SOUL - with rich offerings and adornments?

5. What if we allow our HEARTS to BREAK OPEN WIDE and let
those PRISONERS OF LIES out?

6. The OPENING of the HEART releases a tension, allowing
more FLOW. At first, a GUSH. Then the GENTLE, RHYTHMIC
PULSE begins. Actually, SAVING us.

7. We may find our VALUABLES there, wrapped in beautiful
papers. The GIVERS, arms stretched out for lifetimes.
WAITING.

8. Perhaps the HEART BREAK is the ONLY WAY to FIND our TRUE SELF, ATTACHED to the other side of our LIFE GIVING UMBILICAL CORD.

9. Whose FACE will we see?

10. The CUT was made, long ago. Was the HEART closed or BROKEN?

11. What if it was LOVE that LET US GO?

12. Perhaps all those BROKEN HEARTS are really LOVE leading us to our TRUE SOUL, our true CENTER.

13. Is the CONNECTION ever actually SEVERED? Or is our JOURNEY of BROKEN HEARTS actually the PATHWAY to our source?

14. Upon FINDING OURSELVES, there WILL BE countless others whose HEARTS have been longing to be BROKEN OPEN, too.

15. Oh, WHAT A DAY!

It's Sunday. Another day to love. Happy Sunday

Sunday Morning Ramblings: May 2018

1. I watched the royal wedding.

2. I know. You're surprised. lol

3. I posted yesterday that I loved LOVE.

4. Surprised again. Right?

5. See. This is the thing about Love; capital "L" - of course. The feeling, the simple feeling of love joins more people together than any other feeling OR thought on this planet...and I'm guessing as far reaching as the entire Universe; capital "U" - of course. #you

6. Love draws us closer, perfects us, makes us whole, but not exclusive. Love is not separate or apart. It's simply not broken...at all...no matter who it is flowing through.

7. When we truly allow Love in we are presently gifted with healing. Period.

8. The ego or brain or thinking or fear tries to rob us of that space of perfection by filling it with the mess of our bitterness. However, the true source of anything worth anything comes from Love.

9. And the most perplexing aspect is that WE ALL either know this or DESIRE to know this...and yet, WE run to and fro...for lifetimes LIFETIMES searching.

10. Love dangles above us all day long, in our waking hours, in our sleep, within every relationship, every fiber of our being.

11. Some of us are willing to absorb all the drops, the splashes, the outpourings of Love and become fully saturated so that one gentle squeeze and we are extracting Love without any formal distilling process. Because Love is actually free...

12. ...as in, FREE.

13. Oh, I know. I've given Love to people, situations and they've tried to tarnish it. I've been hurt deeply by loads of people - family, friends, acquaintances. I've cried rivers. I've wanted to hold onto my Love and never share it again.

14. We simply cannot. Love can never be contained. It's available in an endless supply whether we want it or PRETEND not to.

15. So. In order to receive Love, we simply MUST GIVE IT.

It's Sunday Another day to love. Happy Sunday

Unity is strength. Division is weakness.

Swahili Proverb

June

Sunday Morning Ramblings: June 2018

I will never take sides. However, I will always sit with you. And you. And you. And you. Always.
*warning: "heart on sleeve" or the pavement, depending on what time of the day it is

1. I'm simply going to be me. #enjoytheride

2. I wept last night with the force of one of the earth's most fierce waterfalls. It appeared out of nowhere; these tears.

3. Then I remembered.

4. I miss my dad.

5. I miss all the days or times or summer evenings or autumn starlit nights where there may have been conversation, surrounded by laughter and good food, steaming hot coffee, music - just a little pickin' on the guitar, his melodic voice and cascading yodel, the rich conversations about God, those goofy jokes, and the sound of his laughter like my favorite familiar song whisking me away to my childhood, his heart of love, the sweet smiles, warm embraces, loving on my sons, the yumyum sounds as he bit into a muffin or cake, his special connection to

my husband - like brothers from a time gone by, his creative adventurous ideas, all the things we could do together, all the joys we could share with one another, all the missed days...they're adding up so fast now...all the days of the last 17 years minus a few birthdays thrown in with a few "good weather" visits here or at his place.

6. My dad isn't gone from this earth.

7. He left our lives.

8. His pain is that great - to forfeit love and relationship - it is a gaping hole.

9. Our demons appear so big, so tyrannical.

10. Love reminds us that they are paper tigers. When Love enters in all those broken bits, torn edges, rips, and tears in our hearts and souls can be mended.

11. But what if we reach out in love and the other person refuses to take our hand, ignores our call of love? What then?

12. What if we have nothing to do with their great pain except sit present as a reminder of all their mistakes and caused sorrows? What happens then?

13. How does this heart, my heart, let him go?

14. Is hanging onto hope part of the cure or enraging the wound?

15. I feel so alone. I feel so left behind. And yet, I am neither.

16. I simply grasp these rocks and hang here as the water blasts about until a moment when I can hold on no longer. I let go and become one with the rush, slipping fast into the pool below where I can try to swim ashore

finally

catching my breath.

It's Sunday. Another day to love. Happy Sunday.

Holding onto anger is like drinking poison and expecting the other person to die.

Buddha

July

Sunday Morning Ramblings: July 2018

1. What if all ALL TRUE HEALING only happened from within - within a body, a spirit, a family, a nation, a soul?

2. Fixing something is a great skill, if we know what we are doing. But fixing is not healing. Most of us understand this.

3. If we bandage ourselves but never put the needed ointment on the wound and then repeat the behavior, incident, action over again, what then?

4. The wound opens. The wound gets infected. Dirt seeps in. There is hysteria on some level - in the body, the mind, the spirit - individually and/or collectively.

5. If we keep picking at the wound, keep digging into it, keep expressing it, stay constantly focused on it but DO NOTHING meaningful to heal it, the damage spreads. Our system begins to fight - but not to heal; the FIGHT is to SURVIVE.

6. Matters become desperate. Now the entire system's focus is LIFE - staying ALIVE. Not simply LIVING as the result, but NOT DYING.

7. There is an enormous difference between the two. We all have felt this in some way in our lives. What finally happened? Do you remember?

8. I do. I began listening - even when it cost me so much. I began paying attention to my true nature, my true design, that voice within that speaks kindness - which is no easy feat when we are hanging off a cliff, bleeding from our gashes.

9. I began asking myself what went wrong. If we do this, we actually ACTUALLY get answers. Self-examination is one of the most significant actions any of us can do for ourselves if we are to HEAL; heal as an individual, heal as people, heal as a nation.

10. The caveat is that it takes time TIME. Yes, time. But TIME IS AVAILABLE to all of us who ask for help.

11. And not only is it available, but once we begin ASKING ourselves - "How do we heal?" How do we overcome? How do we make life more fulfilling? How do we grow stronger as a person, more autonomous? How do we find our joy again? What are the obstacles?" The ANSWERS arrive. One by one. Not in a rush, not crazed, but in the quiet moments of the self - where EVERYTHING we need to know, to understand is AVAILABLE.

12. This is the beautiful and gracious place where TIME stands still and WAITS for us.

13. It's waiting right now as your world may be crumbling around you.

14. So be BRAVE and begin asking, How do I heal?

15. Your ANSWER will come. It will speak kindly, it will be in the form of a gentle breeze. As you begin to LET GO, you will NOT FALL, you will catch the wind and be carried exactly where you DREAMED and HOPED and BEGGED to go.

16. You will land WITHIN yourself, and while that wound may have left a scar, perhaps your heart beats differently now after it was broken - that loss still an emptiness, there will be something that FILLS you, HEART AND SOUL.

17. It will be YOU - simply because you asked.

18. He or She is waiting.

It's Sunday Another day to love Happy Sunday

Love is a great beautifier.

Louise May Alcott

August

Sunday Morning Ramblings: August 2018

1. It's been a few Sundays, hasn't it?

2. Well, as the Universe would have it as we did our part, several loose ends have been tied, some have become more unraveled and others completely out of our control have brushed up against our faces and our hearts dangling in the soft breeze capturing our spirits, moving us in a direction we would have never dreamed. #foundfamily #brother #sister #cousins

3. A memory from 5 years ago flashed in my mind the other day. As I lay in a heap on the floor after our family's discovery of an awful lie and horrible loss I cried out to God, "What will I do with all of this love?" The Universe replied, "I'm going to send you so many people to love! Just wait!"

4. Waiting is hard. Waiting is long.

5. When the waiting is over the clouds graciously bow allowing the bluest sky you have ever seen to makes itself known.

6. The sun glistens like a flawless dancer performing above just for you and those you love.

7. The birdsong, a special melody, is composed for those who were alongside you in the wait, sitting in a distant audience with hope to be filled. The music crescendos as your spirits find each other at the peak realizing you've been waiting for the same song.

8. A new music fills your heart.

9. It sounds like nothing you've ever known and yet its rhythm becomes familiar as you step in time. This time. The present...

10. ...where all the true gifts are...

11. ...where all the true givers are...

12. ...where all of life is actually fully lived...

13. ...with each other, for each each other.

14. The field is wild. So why not run through it?

15. Just to see what you may find.

It's Sunday Another day to love. Happy Sunday

Goodness is the only investment that never fails.

Henry David Thoreau

September

Sunday Morning Ramblings: September 2018

1. Is the life we want the life we get to live? Or is life simply happening for us and we're just picking up debris, planting flowers, baking bread, screaming inside?

2. Besides the usual rambling, I'm pondering. Or is it the usual pondering and I'm rambling?

3. What defines our life?

4. I believe I'm tied in knots lately.

5. As I try slipping one frayed edge out of its misery, only to find I've tightened the knot further, I remind myself that the answers will come with loosening effect and I WILL once again dangle in the breeze.

6. I will dangle in the breeze.

7. I will dangle in the breeze.

8. In the breeze there is relief.

9. Get to the breeze. Period.

10. I counsel myself. Practice. Practice. Practice.

11. I vacillate between flinging the doors wide open, jumping in both feet or quietly tip-toeing as if my presence will be too colorful, too much for the world around me to cope with. It is certain there will be color and there will be much. When great change occurs people leave us. They've left me. And I've left them. It's hurtful yet understandable. Shifts cause a stir. The energy moves this way and that and we find ourselves haunted by the ghosts of those we loved...gave to...laughed with...prayed for...gave our truth to.

12. What shall I do?

13. I'm on the precipice - with a door in front of me. Is it simply a door? Or is it the cliff's edge...

14. ...with the answer leaning into the sky?

It's Sunday Another day to love Happy Sunday

Sunday Morning Ramblings: September 2018

1. Somewhere along the line, our lifeline, someone or perhaps a few people told us, "You can't do that!"

2. Somewhere along the line, our lifeline, someone or perhaps a few people told us, You CAN do that!"

3. Which one are we holding onto as our personal belief?

4. It's Autumn. Time to let go. Time to change our colors! And drop a few dead leaves.

5. It may be time for you, too.

6. This weekend as I worked and planned for the grand (official) opening of my counseling practice I was reminded of those voices. Some have such a stronghold. But the faint sound of that still small voice is so rich with melodic tones...I weep.

7. Going forward on a hiking trail can be exhilarating, challenging, exhausting, restful, and triumphant.

8. My official credentials have found a spot on the wall in my studio. My authentic credentials reside in my heart and soul.

9. Finding our lost love can be the most beautiful gift we EVER give ourselves.

10. To hold our true self and let LOVE in, let LOVE dance, let LOVE become once again WHO WE ARE is like the beauty of fresh air, the awe of deep hues, the warmth of the autumnal sun.

11. We slow down during this season - the one of change - just long enough to listen to our true voice speaking...

12. ...the one voice that has been drowned out by the cacophony of idle chatter-matter. Yet, it sits still and waits...

13. And when we feel the hum of that voice again, the warmth we seek in life we actually find. The sound of rustling leaves remind us that change is coming, our center becomes stirred.

14. We gather and harvest the goodness we hunger for.

15. We remember that new beginnings are allowed no matter where we are in this life - and just on the horizon of our peace and joy and exhilaration our soul comes running.

16. The reunion, divine!

It's Sunday. Another day to love. Happy Sunday.

Sunday Morning Ramblings: September 2018

1. This building, my studio, represents BUILDING...not simply the art of craftsmanship - although that is, indeed, something to be in awe of - but picking up pieces, sorting them out while sweat and tears - buckets of them - run down our faces as we BEGIN constructing what LOVE says we are...

2. ...from the ground floor up...WHO we have always been - WHAT we were designed for.

3. It is NEVER wholly what WE THINK. This was to be a place for painting and writing...and it was and will remain that.

4. With each slap of color on canvas, every scratch of lead on paper, every heart-filled day of creating with music and meditation and prayer I was being drawn out, a sketch of my

TRUE SELF on a page alongside POETRY and STORY as though I NEVER truly knew myself at all.

5. CREATION CREATES. It does for us what we try to control but can never honestly master. If ALLOWED, the image on the paper comes into VIEW. The words are CLEARLY UNDERSTOOD. We MAY just get a glimpse into WHO WE ARE. With HEARTS OPEN, WIDE EYES and a WILLINGNESS to wait, the DAY arrives.

6. KEEP PLUGGING AWAY. Traversing, bushwhacking in bad shoes, up grassy gnarly knolls, in nasty weather, heart pounding in our chests, through NARROW passageways we cannot YET see the vista. We simply KNOW it is there. We feel it in our SOULS.

7. THE VIEW MAY NOT BE THE TOP. Along the path, there are reminders - kindness, love, friends, family, neighbors, stories, song, gifts, conversation, invitations, a gentle touch, a whisper...we know our path is FULL of what is RICH in LIFE. We JOURNEY on. This is yet another PART of our TRAVELS; another STEP on our LIFE's footpath.

8. GOING SOMEWHERE INSTEAD OF ARRIVING AT OUR DESTINATION. With all the heartbreak, all the loss, all the pain, and deep sadness...in the dark painful days somehow SOMEHOW the LIGHT has the FINAL SAY. The LAMP goes

with us. Build the studio. Paint. Write. Create. Pray. Love.
Listen.

9. STAY WHO YOU ARE. If we FIND OURSELVES and we have
not been altered by FEAR but decide to BUILD based on LOVE -
which is our TRUE NATURE - we DISCOVER TREASURE.

10. THE TREASURE IS YOU. There is nothing more authentic
than AUTHENTICITY. What do you LOVE? What makes YOUR
HEART SING? What FILLS YOU, DRAWS YOU OUT of that box
you've been captured in --- as YOUR EYES REMAIN FIXED on
the OPEN DOOR?

11. My studio has an outside DOOR. As we were in the
planning stages the contractor suggested a door on our addition.
I remember that meeting so vividly. A door? I questioned. He
went on to explain, etc. I turned to EC and we KNEW in that
instant. YES! Indeed! A DOOR! It was a RICH METAPHOR!

12. WE DON'T ALWAYS UNDERSTAND THE DEEPER
MEANING...at first. Thinking about THE DOOR, I considered
how LOVELY it would be to walk out into the yard, the gardens,
the gathering place on our deck...it NEVER occurred to me that
ANYONE would be WALKING IN.

13. LET LOVE WALK IN. Keep your INNER DOORS OPEN.
OPEN your HEART to what LIFE has for YOU. If some DOORS
close or SLAM SHUT, those aren't YOUR DOORS.

14. KEEP IN MIND - your OPEN MIND - that with those OPEN DOORS you may just WALK RIGHT INTO YOUR TRUE SELF - the one who sits waiting at the gate. We NEED that YOU.

15. YES! That TRUE YOU - the one beyond the door.

It's Sunday. Another day to love. Happy Sunday.

Intuition is a spiritual faculty and does not explain, but simply points the way.

Florence Scovel Shinn

October

Sunday Morning Ramblings: October 2018

1. We believe it is our pain that defines us. Perhaps those definitions are like the details of the most beautiful sculpture of ourselves, using our own chisel to complete the process of creation, never allowing anyone else to finish our masterpiece.

2. Then it depends on where we allow the LIGHT to shine on those particular spaces.

3. I've been in the fire. Several in fact. I've also been in a heap on the floor for months. I've lost everything...and almost myself.

4. Through all of that, LOVE and LIGHT never left me.

5. In fact, LOVE has become me.

6. Our brokenness can be the means to an end awakening us to another self---our true self. #bebrave

7. Never be afraid to love. Even if we begin by loving the butterfly first, or the caterpillar, or the wind. Love something. Anything.

8. It is a guarantee we will heal, and love again.

9. And what about trust? Time.

10. My husband and I began searching for his birth mother.

11. We found an abundance of LOVE, just waiting to be poured out, from inside the hearts and souls of the most gorgeous people. #sister #brother #niece #nephew #cousins #family

12. Love shows up.

13. We must keep up the search.

14. Why? Because we deserve to love deeper than the ocean itself.

It's Sunday. Another day to love. Happy Sunday.

Sunday Morning Ramblings: October 2018

1. Loss.

2. Great loss.

3. Love.

4. Great love.

5. If in these tragic moments our hate rises we have nothing. Nothing at all.

6. Love joins the ripped ligaments and sinew of one's soul and WITH BOTH HANDS ties those broken bits to its own.

7. Healing begins WITH each other.

8. We never heal alone.

9. We must carry the injured...

10. ...with tear-soaked dampness allowing the warmth of our breath to blanket this world gone cold.

11. I am here for you. I will never run.

12. My heart will heal with yours.

13. My life will be with yours.

14. My spirit is an offering.

15. I will carry you with me in the soft spots of my being and you will NEVER BE LEFT in fear again.

It's Sunday. Another day to love. Happy Sunday.

Only the wisest and stupidest of men never change.

Confucius

november

Sunday Morning Ramblings: November 2018

1. Today, I'm going to be all over the place.

2. Because today, I am all over the place.

3. Ramblings.

4. I went away. Then I came back. Changed. #VirginiaisforWAYmorethanlovers

5. Follow your soul. It will take you to the most gorgeous places....ever. Unexpectedly, if you can be BE in the moment the GIFTS are there. They really aren't anywhere else. Not in our imagination. Not in tomorrow or next week. But right now. This moment.

6. I need reminders.

7. I still love LOVE people.

8. Listening to my guys+ jam for their demo recording right now. #bestillmyheart #talentedandgoodsouls

9. Never regret being a GOOD PERSON even if the not-nice-people are kicking dirt as you stumble to the ground. I've been there by people who said they LOVED me and were my friends/family/church.

10. I survived WITHOUT guilt/apology/shame/hate. So be good. Be true. You'll get up again and dust yourself off. Guaranteed. #allmylove

11. Love is proof of every single unanswered question, every dilemma, every confusing situation... everything.

12. If we have LOVE, we have everything.

13. What is LOVE?

14. I'd answer that with one word: TRUTH.

15. If we hide or lie or manipulate, we do NOT have love or truth.

16. And now they're playing, Every Breath You Take...I may weep. Oh Gordon Sumner, Andy Summers, Stewart Copeland, if you could meet these people of mine. #tears

17. One day several years ago he asked, "Mom, what music speaks to you and changes you, saves you?

18. Read #15 #thepolice #sting

19. Time and memory in a beautiful dance.

20. My guy is finishing up the details, the trim, today in our bedroom. I'm so grateful for this man. He suffers greatly and still manages to take care of house projects. #CBDcream

21. If we don't change, we remain the same. Are you happy with the same? #GrowthBringsUsClosertotheLIGHT

It's Sunday. Another day to love. Happy Sunday.

No matter how hard the past is, you can always begin again.
Buddha

December

Sunday Morning Ramblings: December 2018

1. I love beginnings.

2. Ironically, I love endings, too. Not all endings. However, even in the endings I'd prefer not to participate in, I find myself on the precipice of possibility with a different view.

3. I love different views, too.

4. We have choices in how we proceed with the endings, the beginnings, and the different views.

5. This year has been full of choices, endings, and new beginnings and different views.

6. We are stronger than we realize.

7. We are more capable than we even know.

8. Until those endings show up forcing new beginnings we may never get out of the bondage of our self, our ego, our broken heart, and dare I say, our weak lost souls.

9. You know your soul is weak if you have no joy; if anger or sadness is your go-to emotion.

10. This weakened state is not who you are. It is a veil or straight jacket or cage. Either covered or flying around a small room calling it freedom, is not a soul saved. It is a soul trapped.

11. I pray for your freedom. I pray for walls to crumble, for people to awaken, for the keys to be handed to you in any way possible.

12. These happenings shake us --- loose.

350

13. And then the person you become is the person WE ALL need. It is the person, the soul, we long to know.

14. It is the person you've been longing to know. You've been crying out for her, him for far too long.

15. Then YOU, the TRUE YOU, the lovely YOU, the BRAVE YOU is born.

16. And that beautiful pearl is found.

17. Such a soulful ending, such a heartfelt beginning...

18. I pray.

It's Sunday. Another day to love. Happy Sunday

2019

How very little can be done under the spirit of fear.

Florence Nightingale

April

Sunday Morning Ramblings: April 2019

1. When your inner spirit tells you to do something, honor that. It will never NEVER steer you in the wrong direction.

2. If God tells you to do something, honor that. He will never NEVER steer you in the wrong direction. #samething #peopleoftheLIGHT

3. As some of you may recall, several years ago I left an entire group of people I loved dearly because that voice VOICE of LOVE was so strong. We were saved from something very VERY WRONG. Be brave not only for yourself but for the hope of others because TRUE LOVE is ACTUALLY THAT STRONG. #bebrave

4. Mountains move. #proof

5. We are connected in ways we cannot even begin to understand. I sensed a deep sadness in an actor that I had been watching a few days ago. In fact, she's a British comedian. Her show was on British TV years ago (I needed to laugh! She is so funny!!). I walked around for 3 days carrying this sadness that was related to her, I didn't try to shake it. I went outside for a walk and looked up at the sky and prayed for her. I sent out that

prayer of love to her through the sky over to Great Britain (I live in upstate New York). Then out of the blue, I had the idea to look her up on FB and Twitter. I'd never looked her up before. She had just posted that she'd had a rough 3 days - writing that we all have them and she needed a perspective change. She wrote that she went outdoors and looked up at the sky and felt better. (she posted several photos of the sky on her page) Wow! These connections are powerful. Whenever this depth happens for me I feel gratitude overflowing inside and out. It changes my life...for the better. #thepowerofconnection

6. Never NEVER discount those deep feelings, yearnings, sensings. Reach out if you can. Tapping into that omnipotent power will open doors for you... to your heart, your soul, some beautiful connection. #reachout

7. I love my guys.

8. These are ramblings.

9. Some days it's not easy being me...frizzy hair, tall and sometimes awkward, heart on my sleeve nearly every FREAKIN MINUTE, poetry at every turn.

10. Then other days I am so utterly in LOVE and in AWE of the human being I am.

11. Today is that day. #rise

12. Being you THE TRUE YOU lends a force of vulnerability and transparency that will make some run away. BUT THOSE WHO RUN TOWARD YOU have within themselves the POWER OF THE RADIANT SUN. Sit with those people whenever you can.

13. I'm so happy Spring is here. Our walkway to my gorgeous creative studio is almost complete. #coloredstonepath

14. Fear is a force. LOVE IS STILL MORE POWERFUL. #LOVE

15. I woke up early this morning and wrapped Easter/Passover gifts for my sons. I'm still that mother. #creator #lover #riser

16. Spiders have a story. #forreals #savethem #putthemoutdoors #thankyouverymuch #abeautifultwoyearoldtaughtmethis #IamchangedffFOREVER #secondson

17. Being sensitive is ACTUALLY a SUPER POWER!

18. Now, go RISE! Then, ROLL BACK your stone and MOVE that mountain!!

It's Sunday. Another day to love. Happy Sunday

Those who don't move won't notice their chains.

unknown

may

Sunday Morning Ramblings: May 2019

1. It is our pain that bridges the power of compassion and hope, if we are awake enough on our journey to take notice.

2. Cross that bridge or burn it. Either way, we can choose to heal.

3. I love my job.

4. One oppressive energy in the room or in our lives creates a darkness we may not know how to escape from until it or they are gone or we go into a new room or leave the building. #metaphorandrealpeople

5. Ramblings. Short.

6. Maybe sweet.

7. Most likely, real.

It's Sunday. Another day to love. Happy Sunday

The world breaks everyone and afterward, some are strong at the broken places.

Ernest Hemingway

August

Sunday Morning Ramblings: August 2019

1. I was going outdoors for a ramble this morning but stopped in my tracks to ramble here instead… for a bit.

2. The world needs something. Something much more tangible than a simple prayer. The world needs truth seekers, not religious seekers… REAL TRUTH SEEKERS.

3. The men and women who stand up for TRUTH.

4. It's not an easy position to be in, you realize?

5. I ramble...see this is exactly how I do this. I feel moved and sit down and begin typing...what I feel, see, sense. It is NOT and NEVER has been planned or contrived.

6. So I realized this very second as I typed #4 that today is the 6 YEAR ANNIVERSARY of the day my husband and sons and I stood up for TRUTH. Then we WALKED OUT. Left a LIE so deep and dark. Honestly, you can't make this stuff up...and why would any of us ever want to? Life holds so much VOLUME. Today is that anniversary.

7. I don't think much about the people or the arrogance anymore until I "see" it somewhere else on the earth.

8. It is a DARK FORCE, AN EVIL. It walks the earth as an energy and "devours who it may."

9. Pay attention to "who it may." That means the dark energy is ALLOWED, perhaps even INVITED IN.

10. Walking out of *that building,* trusting the essence of Love's spirit within us was one of the BRAVEST THINGS a person or persons could do. We did so without knowing what was behind the curtain. We didn't "see" it with our eyes. We FELT it in our SOULS.

11. What is your SOUL feeling right now? Is there something you NEED to STAND UP FOR AND THEN WALK AWAY FROM?

12. It won't be easy. These TRUE things in life NEVER ARE.

13. But if WE do NOT stand up, then we deny our SOUL, our ESSENCE. What would LIFE be for if we allowed that? The ONLY answer is the finite manner of existence of materialism and ego. In other words, a LIFE VOID OF REAL LOVE, REAL CONNECTION, REAL HEALING, REAL RELATIONSHIP.

14. I used to think we NEEDED TO UNDERSTAND everything in this LIFE.

15. No. Not anymore.

16. We NEED to TRUST our DIVINITY. Our INTUITION. Our GUT. Our TRUTH. Call it whatever you need to.

17. The NAME of it isn't where the power is. The ACTION you take in that LEAP OF FAITH is what CHANGES THE WORLD, HEALS THE WORLD, HELPS THE WORLD, HEALS YOUR BROKEN TO BITS BLEEDING HEART.

18. Liars stand on stages, platforms all over this planet and shout names in accusations and shout names with false humility. And yet their evil spirits persist to harm millions.

19. TRUST your SOUL. TRUST that LEAP OF FAITH.

20. It's the ONLY way to FLY and then LAND ON THE TRUEST FORM OF SOLID GROUND.

It's Sunday. Another day to love. Happy Sunday.

Sunday Morning Ramblings: August 2019

1. So here I am. Again.

2. Sitting on one of many of life's steep cliffs.

3. Do I leap? Or walk across the street to the University and get a job?

4. Am I art?

5. It's all I have...well not really. But wait. Yes, it is.

6. It is not, however, all I need. This is the conundrum.

7. This crossroad is poignant, not desperate. So many crossroads in my life have been desperate.

8. I've been homeless. I've been without a job, without money. I've been homeless without a job or money. I know, it's startling even to me to acknowledge that imbalance in my life. I was younger. But age has nothing to do with the sadness, confusion, fear attached. Those emotions are tight; tucked deep inside. Breaths held like an 18-wheeler is barreling next to you on the highway, the powerful urge to close your eyes almost overtakes you until the 40-ton vehicle passes. You pray it passes. Then you breathe.

9. So as I'm finishing my book, working on FTFP, meeting with businesses, the community, counseling, etc. lingering in the background is our old "friend", Doubt, chumming it up with our other "friend", Failure. Across the table is Fear and sitting next to him is Lost Hope. And. They're all laughing, pointing fingers.

10. As a kid, I was made fun of...a lot. I don't tell you this for your sympathy. Although many of you I know here personally will pour out care after reading that. Thank you. I write that memory because since a child I have heard those voices in the backdrop of life.

11. They never got the best of me. They never knew me.

12. They don't know us.

13. Read that one again. THEY DON'T KNOW US.

14. In our vulnerability, our leaps of faith, we either jump or we don't.

15. My leaping will never look like yours. Your leaps will never look like mine.

16. When I used to take any job I could find because I never got a college degree I'd be satisfied. I could eat. Pay my bills. Most of them.

17. And, interestingly enough, I never felt poor.

18. The soul knows the richness and values in life. But we must MUST pay attention to it speaking. Listen to it, in the silence. Hear what it has to say.

19. Nearly twenty years ago I left my very good job at the university to try my hand at being a SAHM (Stay-At-Home-Mom). It's all I was. It's all I could do. It did NOT, however, bring in a single cent to our household.

20. After we woke up and realized that we contributed so much money to a cause that was faulty, to say the least, I did have moments where I wished I'd stayed at my job.

21. Was it the "right" decision? It was at the time.

22. Pouring one's heart and soul and everything I had into raising two human beings is and will remain truly my greatest accomplishment - even without the best dental plan, 401K, free tuition, pay raises, promotions, and accolades.

23. I know this is long...ramblings.

24. So as I embark on this next journey, I will give it my all; my heart, my soul, my spirit, my time. And I will be afraid.

25. And. I will be brave.

It's Sunday. Another day to love. Happy Sunday.

Art and life really are the same, and both can only be about a spiritual journey, a path towards a reunion with a supreme creator, with god, with the divine; and this is true no matter how unlikely, how strange, how unorthodox, one's particular life path might appear to one's self or others at any given moment.

Genesis P-Orridge

With Gratitude

To the man I married. You are a fixed rock in my wall of life. I love you, forever.

To my sons who gave *me* life the day you were born. I love you.

To my older brother, Zain. When I said I didn't know if I should write, you replied, "Write and never stop!" I love you.

To my sister, Jenelle, I love you. You are a capable, amazing pearl.

To my Gram who left the earth a long time ago, but managed to teach me that if a pigeon lands on your head simply walk down the street with your feathered adornment and wear it proud. Thank you, my lovely, Hungarian, high-ball drinking, braless sage of a grandmother.

Mom, for finding those black sneakers and every other sacrifice. I love you.

Dad, for playing along when I told everyone you grew your armpit hair long enough for braids. And for being the taxi for me and my friends at all hours. I'll love you forever.

To my nieces, I loved you from the first day I met you. Nothing will ever change that.

To all my friends here in town, all over the country and the world. Our times together are how the light dances through the mosaic of my life. I love you.

To all the friends I carry within-authors, poets, storytellers, teachers, songwriters, monks, counselors. You poured from your cup, liquid wisdom that quenches my soul. You saved me. Thank you for breathing out your stories, giving me life.

To my sister-in-law, Lori, for marrying my brother and helping me here with all these words. I love you, Pea!

Sissy, I found my zen. Love you all. So happy we found each other. And all the beautiful cousins. Allan, you rock!

To Sue and Greg, Emily and Dustin, Nathan, Patrick, Lauren and Jocelyn for being family and the healing balm I needed. Love you all.

To Julie whose one-liners can part the red sea – making a way for those to get across, should they choose. Love you, girlfriend.

To my neighbors, in our sweet neighborhood, who carried me through such a broken time. Whether you knew it or not, your kindness healed my hope in community. Thank you.

To God/Universe/Spirit, for all of it.
I dance, sing & twirl in awe!

Other Particulars

There are a few places where I borrowed definitions of words or historical events. They are from my MacBook Pro dictionary.

The page breaks are beautiful and poignant quotes from freedom and love seekers, songwriters and composers, authors and poets, artists and scientists, each attributed by name. Other than that, all the other words are mine, to the best of my knowledge, written in the moment as I rambled.

Betsy, you are a ROCK STAR!

Contact Information

If you're interested in contacting me, please find me through FreeToFindPearls on Facebook.

I'm available for Book Signings & Speaking Engagements, Finding Your Pearl Workshops & Intuitive Art Workshops, SOUL Clinic Counseling
&
FreeToFindPearls
Music Performances.

And finally this

Love and say it with your life.
St. Augustine of Hippo

What is done in love is done well.
Vincent Van Gogh

Notes:

Made in the USA
Middletown, DE
15 February 2020